Introduction: Setting the Stage for Wealth Building

Acknowledgments and Author Bio
Pg. 293

Setting the Stage for Wealth Building

Chapter Content

The pursuit of wealth is a journey that transcends mere financial accumulation; it's a path toward achieving a life of freedom, security, and fulfillment. In a world where financial well-being can greatly impact our quality of life, this book serves as your guide to mastering the art of wealth creation. In these pages, you'll embark on a journey to discover the principles, strategies, and mindset required to not only build wealth but to master it.

Introduction: The Call of Financial Well-Being

Picture this: a life where you have the freedom to make choices based on your desires and dreams, rather than financial constraints. Imagine waking up every day with a sense of security, knowing that you've taken the necessary steps to safeguard your future. Envision the joy of giving back to the community and leaving a lasting legacy for generations to come. These aspirations, shared by many, are the foundations of our quest for wealth.

Yet, for so many, these dreams remain elusive, overshadowed by the daily grind of financial stress, debt, and uncertainty. The pursuit of wealth is not merely a desire for material possessions; it's a yearning for a life of abundance, purpose, and peace. This book is your compass on the journey toward that life.

The Essence of Wealth

Before we dive into the practical strategies and techniques of wealth building, let's reflect on the essence of wealth. Wealth is not just about accumulating money; it's a multifaceted concept that encompasses various aspects of life. It includes financial wealth, but it also extends to emotional well-being, health, relationships, and personal growth.

Think of wealth as a symphony, with each instrument representing a different facet of your life. The goal is to create harmony, ensuring that your financial wealth aligns with your overall well-being. A holistic approach to wealth considers not only how much money you have but how it contributes to your happiness, security, and fulfillment.

The Key Themes of This Book

As we journey together, several key themes will emerge:

1. **The Power of Mindset:** Your mindset plays a pivotal role in your ability to create and maintain wealth. We'll explore how beliefs, attitudes, and habits shape your financial reality and how you can cultivate a wealth mindset.

2. **Goal Setting and Planning:** Clear goals and a well-structured financial plan are the foundation of wealth creation. We'll guide you through the process of setting meaningful goals and creating a roadmap for your financial success.

3. **Income Generation:** Whether through your career, entrepreneurship, or investments, increasing your income is a critical step toward building wealth. We'll delve into strategies to boost your earning potential.

4. **Smart Saving and Investing:** Making informed decisions about saving and investing is essential. We'll demystify financial markets and guide you in making prudent investment choices.

6

5. **Debt Management:** Effective debt management is often an overlooked aspect of wealth building. We'll discuss strategies for reducing debt and achieving financial freedom.

6. **Diversification:** Relying on a single income source is risky. We'll explore the concept of building multiple income streams for greater financial security.

7. **Legacy and Philanthropy:** Building wealth isn't just for your benefit; it's an opportunity to leave a lasting legacy and make a positive impact on the world.

The Journey to Wealth Mastery

Consider this book as a roadmap for your journey to wealth mastery. As you navigate these pages, you'll encounter stories of individuals who started with humble beginnings but achieved financial success through determination, smart choices, and a wealth mindset.

We'll provide you with practical tools, actionable steps, and valuable insights to help you make informed financial decisions. But remember, the journey is as important as the destination. Along the way, you'll learn, grow, and evolve—developing not only your wealth but also yourself.

So, are you ready to embark on this transformative journey toward wealth mastery? Let's set the stage for a life of financial well-being, abundance, and fulfillment.

Chapter 1: Defining Wealth

Define what wealth means beyond just money.

Wealth, in its purest form, encompasses an abundance of not just financial resources but also a rich tapestry of experiences, knowledge, relationships, and well-being. It is the sum of our achievements, aspirations, and contentment in life. Beyond the material, wealth encompasses the freedom to pursue one's passions, the ability to provide for loved ones, and the capacity to make a positive impact on the world. This broader perspective on wealth urges us to recognize the immeasurable value of our time, health, and the intangible moments that add depth and richness to our existence.

Furthermore, wealth extends its reach into the emotional and psychological realms of our lives. It involves a profound sense of security, peace of mind, and the liberation from the constant worry about financial survival. True wealth grants us the ability to make choices that align with our values and desires, whether it's exploring new horizons, dedicating time to personal growth, or giving back to society. It is the feeling of fulfillment that arises when our life's purpose aligns with our financial resources, creating a harmonious symphony of prosperity that resonates with our innermost aspirations.

In the journey to redefine wealth beyond monetary measures, we unlock a world of possibilities, where the pursuit of financial success converges with the pursuit of a life rich in meaning, purpose, and fulfillment. It is through this holistic understanding of wealth that we embark on a transformative journey, one that empowers us to master the art of wealth in all its dimensions.

Exploring the Psychological and Emotional Aspects of Wealth

In our relentless pursuit of wealth, we frequently find ourselves consumed by the tangible metrics that define financial success—bank balances, assets, investments, and material possessions. Yet, as we embark on a deeper exploration of wealth, we uncover a truth that transcends these monetary markers. True wealth, we soon discover, is not confined to the realm of numbers and possessions; it extends its reach into the intricate landscapes of our minds and hearts, weaving a complex tapestry that encompasses the psychological and emotional dimensions of our lives.

A Broader Canvas of Wealth

To define wealth comprehensively, we must first acknowledge that it is a multifaceted concept, a spectrum that ranges far beyond the confines of currency notes and coins. At its core, wealth represents the totality of our existence, the sum of our experiences, knowledge, relationships, and well-being. It is the intricate interplay between the tangible and intangible elements that compose our lives.

Wealth, in its most profound sense, is not a mere accumulation of assets; it is the embodiment of abundance in all its forms. It is the sum of our achievements, aspirations, and contentment. It is the freedom to pursue our passions, the capacity to provide for our loved ones, and the ability to make a meaningful impact on the world. In this expansive definition of wealth, we find ourselves appreciating the intrinsic value of our time, health, and the precious moments that breathe depth and richness into our existence.

Beyond the material, wealth unfurls its branches into the emotional and psychological terrain of our lives. It encompasses a profound sense of security and peace of mind, liberating us from the perpetual burden of financial worry. True wealth grants us the autonomy to make choices that resonate with our values and desires—whether it involves embarking on new adventures, dedicating time to personal growth, or engaging in acts of generosity and philanthropy. It is the feeling of fulfillment that arises when our life's purpose harmoniously aligns with our financial resources, creating a symphony of prosperity that resonates with our innermost aspirations.

Yet, in our contemporary pursuit of wealth, the psychological and emotional dimensions often take a back seat to the relentless pursuit of material gain. In this chapter, we shall delve into the intricacies of these often-neglected facets of wealth, exploring the profound impact they have on our overall well-being and our ability to master the art of wealth.

Wealth and the Mind: The Psychological Underpinnings

Our journey into the psychological aspects of wealth begins with the understanding that our relationship with money and abundance is deeply rooted in the recesses of our minds. Our thoughts, beliefs, and attitudes towards wealth play a pivotal role in shaping our financial reality.

At its core, the concept of wealth is subjective, and it varies from person to person. For some, wealth may be synonymous with opulence, while for others, it may be defined by financial security and stability. These varying perceptions of wealth are often shaped by our early experiences, upbringing, cultural influences, and societal norms.

The Money Mindset

Central to our understanding of wealth is the notion of the "money mindset." This mindset encompasses our beliefs and attitudes towards money and our capacity to generate and manage it effectively. Our money mindset is not static; it evolves over time and can be influenced by external factors such as financial setbacks, economic conditions, or personal experiences.

A healthy money mindset is characterized by a positive and empowering view of money. It fosters a sense of financial abundance and confidence in one's ability to manage resources effectively. Individuals with a healthy money mindset tend to approach financial challenges with resilience and optimism, viewing them as opportunities for growth and learning.

On the contrary, a negative money mindset is often marked by fear, scarcity, and self-limiting beliefs. This mindset can manifest as anxiety about money, chronic worry about financial stability, and a persistent sense of inadequacy. Such beliefs can become self-fulfilling prophecies, hindering one's capacity to accumulate and grow wealth.

The Emotional Quotient of Wealth

Wealth, as we have come to understand, is not merely a matter of numbers; it is also intimately tied to our emotional well-being. Our emotions, in many ways, are the barometers of our financial health, reflecting the ebb and flow of our monetary experiences.

Consider the emotions associated with wealth—happiness, contentment, anxiety, and even guilt. These emotional responses are not just byproducts of financial circumstances; they are intertwined with our financial choices, values, and priorities.

Happiness and Fulfillment

For many, the pursuit of wealth is driven by the aspiration for happiness and fulfillment. Yet, the relationship between wealth and happiness is nuanced. Research in positive psychology has demonstrated that while a certain level of financial stability is crucial for well-being, beyond a certain point, the correlation between wealth and happiness becomes less significant.

This phenomenon is known as the "Easterlin Paradox," which suggests that once basic needs are met, additional wealth does not significantly contribute to overall happiness. Instead, factors such as the quality of relationships, a sense of purpose, and personal growth play a more substantial role in determining one's emotional well-being.

Understanding this paradox prompts us to question the relentless pursuit of material wealth and encourages us to explore alternative sources of happiness and fulfillment. It invites us to consider the role of experiences, connections, and the pursuit of meaning in our lives.

Financial Anxiety and Stress

Conversely, the accumulation of wealth can also be accompanied by financial anxiety and stress. The responsibility of managing substantial assets can lead to a heightened sense of financial pressure and the fear of potential loss. This anxiety can manifest as sleepless nights, strained relationships, and a constant preoccupation with financial matters.

Such financial stress is not limited to those with significant wealth; it can affect individuals across the entire socio-economic spectrum. The fear of financial instability, mounting debts, or the uncertainty of economic downturns can weigh heavily on the psyche.

Managing financial anxiety requires developing resilience and coping strategies. It involves cultivating financial literacy, adopting effective budgeting and saving habits, and seeking support through financial counseling or therapy when needed. The recognition that financial stress is a shared experience, not an individual failing, can be a powerful step towards mitigating its impact.

The Emotional Toll of Wealth: Guilt and Responsibility

As wealth accumulates, it brings with it a sense of privilege and responsibility. Those who have achieved financial success often grapple with feelings of guilt and the weight of societal expectations. They may question whether they deserve their wealth or feel compelled to use it for the greater good.

This emotional complexity is particularly evident in cases of inherited wealth. Heirs of substantial fortunes often find themselves navigating a complex landscape of legacy and responsibility. The burden of preserving and growing family wealth, coupled with the desire to honor the legacy of those who came before, can be emotionally taxing.

In response to these challenges, some individuals embrace philanthropy as a means of channeling their wealth towards meaningful causes. Philanthropy not only addresses the emotional dimensions of wealth but also offers a sense of purpose and fulfillment.

The Ripple Effect of Financial Well-Being

Our exploration of the psychological and emotional aspects of wealth underscores the profound impact of our thoughts and emotions on our financial well-being. It highlights the importance of cultivating a healthy money mindset that fosters financial confidence and resilience.

Moreover, it prompts us to consider the broader implications of wealth on our lives and the lives of those around us. How we manage our wealth, whether it's the financial, mental and emotional, or relational and social dimensions, has a ripple effect that extends far beyond our individual experiences.

Our financial choices, for instance, can impact not only our immediate family but also future generations. Prudent financial planning and responsible stewardship can pave the way for generational wealth transfer, ensuring that our descendants have the resources and opportunities to thrive. Conversely, poor financial management may perpetuate cycles of financial hardship, affecting the well-being of our heirs.

Similarly, our mental and emotional wealth can influence the quality of our relationships and our ability to nurture meaningful connections. A positive mindset and emotional resilience enable us to engage in healthier, more fulfilling relationships, fostering a supportive and harmonious social network. In contrast, unresolved emotional baggage or a negative mindset can strain our interactions, leading to misunderstandings, conflicts, and strained connections.

Furthermore, our relational and social wealth contributes to the strength and vibrancy of our communities and society as a whole. Acts of kindness, generosity, and community engagement have the power to create a positive impact beyond our immediate circle, fostering a culture of empathy, collaboration, and social responsibility. Conversely, neglecting our social connections can lead to a sense of isolation and detachment, both on a personal and societal level.

In essence, our approach to wealth extends far beyond personal gain; it shapes the world in which we live. It underscores our responsibility to consider not only our individual well-being but also the collective welfare of our communities and society.

This holistic perspective on wealth compels us to view wealth mastery as a journey that goes beyond personal enrichment. It encourages us to align our financial choices, our emotional well-being, and our relationships with our values, striving for a balanced and harmonious existence. In doing so, we not only enhance our own lives but also contribute positively to the lives of those around us, leaving a lasting legacy of true wealth—an abundance that transcends mere monetary measures and enriches the human experience.

The Three Dimensions of Wealth

In our quest to comprehend the multifaceted concept of wealth, it becomes evident that wealth is not a monolithic entity defined solely by financial assets. Instead, it reveals itself as a complex, three-dimensional tapestry encompassing the tangible and intangible facets of our existence. To embark on a profound exploration of wealth, we shall categorize it into three primary dimensions, each offering a unique perspective on what it means to be truly rich in life.

1. Financial Wealth: Navigating the Material Realm

The first and most commonly recognized dimension of wealth is the realm of financial abundance. This dimension encompasses the tangible assets and resources that accumulate over the course of our lives. It is the domain of currency notes, bank balances, real estate holdings, investments, and income-generating ventures. Financial wealth equips us with the means to lead comfortable lives, plan for the future, and materialize our financial aspirations.

At the core of financial wealth lies the art of financial stewardship. It involves prudent financial management, including budgeting, saving, investing, and debt management. Financial wealth, in its purest form, bestows upon us the freedom to make choices that align with our financial goals and values. It empowers us to secure our future, provide for our loved ones, and extend our capacity to make a positive impact on the world.

Yet, financial wealth is not merely about accumulating riches; it is also about mastering the art of responsible wealth management. This mastery entails an understanding of financial markets, investment strategies, and risk management. It involves the ability to adapt to changing economic conditions and navigate the complexities of the financial landscape.

Moreover, financial wealth is intrinsically linked to the pursuit of financial goals, which extend beyond the accumulation of assets. Financial goals encompass objectives such as achieving financial independence, retiring comfortably, funding education, and leaving a financial legacy. They serve as guiding beacons on our financial journey, providing direction and purpose.

While financial wealth is undoubtedly a crucial dimension of overall wealth, it is not the sole determinant of our well-being. It is but one thread in the intricate tapestry of our existence, interwoven with the dimensions of mental and emotional wealth, as well as relational and social wealth.

2. Mental and Emotional Wealth: Nurturing the Inner Landscape

The second dimension of wealth introduces us to the rich and complex inner world of our thoughts, emotions, and psychological well-being. This dimension, often overlooked in conventional definitions of wealth, is a cornerstone of our overall quality of life. It encompasses our mental and emotional wealth—a wealth of profound importance that extends far beyond the boundaries of financial assets.

Mental and emotional wealth encompasses a host of qualities and attributes that contribute to our inner richness. At its core lies the cultivation of a positive mindset—an outlook that fosters resilience, optimism, and a deep sense of self-worth. A wealth of emotional intelligence enables us to navigate the complexities of human interactions, manage stress, and foster healthy relationships.

The journey to mental and emotional wealth invites us to explore the treasures of self-awareness and self-compassion. It is a realm where personal growth and self-improvement reign supreme, where we embrace challenges as opportunities for learning, and where we cherish the moments of joy and gratitude that grace our lives.

Resilience, an invaluable facet of mental and emotional wealth, empowers us to face life's inevitable setbacks with fortitude and grace. It is the capacity to bounce back from adversity, to view failures as stepping stones to success, and to maintain our equilibrium in the face of life's trials.

Moreover, mental and emotional wealth encompasses the richness of mindfulness and emotional balance. It is the ability to be fully present in the moment, to savor life's experiences, and to navigate its challenges with grace and composure. This dimension of wealth emphasizes the importance of holistic well-being, acknowledging that our emotional and psychological states profoundly influence our overall health and happiness.

In our pursuit of mental and emotional wealth, we recognize that it is an ongoing journey—a process of continuous self-discovery and growth. It calls us to nurture our inner world with the same care and attention that we devote to our financial well-being. It invites us to invest in practices that promote mental and emotional health, such as meditation, mindfulness, counseling, and the cultivation of positive habits.

The realization of mental and emotional wealth is not just a personal triumph; it radiates outward, influencing our relationships, our interactions with the world, and our capacity to lead fulfilling lives. It adds depth and resonance to the very essence of our existence, reminding us that true wealth extends beyond the material and into the rich tapestry of our inner selves.

3. Relational and Social Wealth: The Value of Human Connection

The third dimension of wealth introduces us to the richness of human connections and the profound impact of our relationships on our overall well-being. This dimension—relational and social wealth—is a testament to the interconnectedness of our lives, highlighting the invaluable wealth we gain through our interactions with others.

Our relationships, whether with family, friends, colleagues, or the broader community, form the intricate fabric of our lives. They offer emotional support during times of difficulty, create a sense of belonging, and provide opportunities for personal growth and collaboration.

At the heart of relational and social wealth is the understanding that our connections with others are not just incidental to our well-being but are, in fact, integral to it. These relationships contribute to our sense of purpose, fulfillment, and overall life satisfaction.

Consider the wealth of a close-knit family, where love, support, and shared experiences create a profound sense of belonging and connection. Think of the wealth of enduring friendships, where laughter, shared memories, and mutual understanding enrich our lives immeasurably. Reflect upon the wealth of mentorship and guidance, where the wisdom of experienced individuals serves as a beacon on our own life journey.

Relational and social wealth is a dynamic dimension that emphasizes the importance of investing in our relationships. It encourages us to cultivate meaningful connections, nurture existing bonds, and contribute positively to our communities. It reminds us that our wealth is not measured solely by what we accumulate for ourselves but also by the impact we have on the lives of others.

Furthermore, this dimension underscores the principle of reciprocity—the idea that the wealth of our relationships is enhanced when we give as well as receive. Acts of kindness, support, and generosity not only enrich the lives of those we touch but also amplify the sense of fulfillment and purpose within us.

In our modern, fast-paced world, where the pursuit of material success often takes precedence, it is easy to overlook the significance of relational and social wealth. Yet, as we explore this dimension, we come to realize that it is an essential source of true abundance—one that transcends monetary measures and adds depth and meaning to our lives.

The Interplay of Dimensions: A Holistic Wealth Perspective

As we navigate the intricate dimensions of wealth—financial, mental and emotional, and relational and social—we begin to perceive the interplay between them. These dimensions are not isolated but interwoven threads in the tapestry of our lives. They influence and shape one another, creating a dynamic synergy that defines our overall well-being.

Consider, for instance, the relationship between financial wealth and mental and emotional wealth. A strong financial foundation can alleviate financial stress and provide the resources necessary for investing in mental and emotional well-being. Conversely, a positive mindset and emotional resilience can enhance our capacity to manage financial challenges and make prudent financial decisions.

Similarly, relational and social wealth plays a pivotal role in our overall wealth equation. Our relationships not only offer emotional support during financial hardships but also open doors to opportunities and collaborations that can bolster our financial well-being. Think of the entrepreneur who builds a successful business through a network of supportive contacts or the professional who advances their career through mentorship and networking.

Furthermore, the synergy among these dimensions extends to our holistic experience of wealth. When financial, mental and emotional, and relational and social wealth are in harmonious alignment, we experience a profound sense of fulfillment and balance in our lives. This equilibrium empowers us to live with purpose, pursue our passions, and make a positive impact on the world while securing our financial future.

In our journey to master the art of wealth, it is essential to recognize that these dimensions are not mutually exclusive but rather intertwined aspects of our existence. A truly prosperous life emerges when we prioritize and nurture each dimension, acknowledging their collective influence on our well-being.

As we continue to explore the multifaceted nature of wealth, we gain a more profound understanding of what it truly means to be wealthy. It transcends the confines of financial assets, delving into the rich landscapes of our inner selves and the meaningful connections we forge with others. This holistic perspective on wealth invites us to embark on a transformative journey—one that empowers us to master the art of wealth in all its dimensions, ultimately leading to a life of true abundance, purpose, and fulfillment.

The Interplay of Wealth Dimensions

In our quest to master the art of wealth, we must delve deeper into the intricate interplay of its dimensions—financial wealth, mental and emotional wealth, and relational and social wealth. These dimensions do not exist in isolation; they are dynamic, interconnected aspects of our lives that influence and shape one another. To fully understand wealth in its multifaceted glory, we must recognize and appreciate the synergies that exist between them.

Financial Wealth and Its Relationship with Other Dimensions

Financial wealth, often the most tangible and quantifiable dimension of wealth, plays a pivotal role in our overall well-being. It provides us with the means to lead comfortable lives, pursue our dreams, and secure our financial future. However, its influence extends far beyond the realm of bank balances and investments.

Consider, for instance, how financial wealth can bolster our mental and emotional well-being. When we have the financial stability to meet our basic needs and plan for the future, we experience a profound sense of security. This security can alleviate financial stress and anxiety, allowing us to focus on personal growth, self-care, and the pursuit of happiness.

Moreover, financial wealth can empower us to make choices that align with our values and aspirations. It provides the freedom to explore new opportunities, whether they involve pursuing higher education, traveling, or dedicating time to meaningful pursuits. These choices, in turn, contribute to our emotional well-being and overall life satisfaction.

Conversely, financial stress and instability can take a toll on our mental and emotional health. The constant worry about making ends meet or coping with debt can lead to anxiety, depression, and strained relationships. In this way, our financial dimension directly influences our mental and emotional dimensions.

Mental and Emotional Wealth: A Catalyst for Financial Success

While financial wealth is undeniably important, it thrives in the presence of mental and emotional wealth. Our mental and emotional well-being forms the bedrock upon which we make financial decisions, navigate challenges, and persevere in the pursuit of our goals.

Consider the role of a positive mindset in financial success. A wealth of optimism and resilience can empower us to view setbacks as opportunities for growth rather than insurmountable obstacles. It encourages us to maintain a long-term perspective, weathering the storms of financial volatility with grace and determination.

Emotional intelligence, another facet of mental and emotional wealth, equips us with the tools to navigate complex financial situations and interpersonal dynamics effectively. It enables us to communicate with empathy, build strong relationships, and make sound financial decisions in both personal and professional contexts.

Furthermore, our mental and emotional well-being directly impacts our financial behaviors. Individuals with a wealth of self-discipline and emotional regulation tend to exhibit better financial habits, such as budgeting, saving, and prudent investing. They are less prone to impulsive spending and more capable of making rational, well-informed financial choices.

In essence, mental and emotional wealth acts as a catalyst for financial success. It fosters the resilience, adaptability, and emotional intelligence needed to thrive in a complex financial landscape. When these dimensions are in harmony, we are better equipped to navigate financial challenges and make prudent decisions that contribute to our long-term financial well-being.

Relational and Social Wealth: Nurturing Our Financial Journey

Beyond the individual dimensions of financial and mental and emotional wealth, there exists a profound interplay with relational and social wealth. Our relationships and social connections have the power to shape our financial journey in significant ways.

Consider the role of a supportive network in financial success. When we have a wealth of genuine relationships, we are more likely to receive emotional support during times of financial difficulty. This support can provide the emotional resilience needed to weather financial storms without succumbing to stress and anxiety.

Furthermore, relational and social wealth can open doors to opportunities that enhance our financial well-being. Strong connections with mentors, peers, and colleagues can lead to collaborations, partnerships, and career advancements that may not have been possible in isolation.

The power of networking, often underestimated in the financial world, is a testament to the value of relational and social wealth. Attending social events, participating in professional organizations, and maintaining meaningful connections can lead to valuable insights, referrals, and access to resources that can bolster our financial success.

Conversely, a lack of social connections or strained relationships can hinder our financial journey. Isolation and a lack of emotional support can magnify the challenges of financial stress and financial decision-making. In such circumstances, individuals may feel overwhelmed and less equipped to navigate financial difficulties effectively.

Moreover, relational and social wealth extends beyond personal connections to the broader community and society. Engaging in acts of kindness, philanthropy, and community service are forms of social wealth that not only contribute to the greater good but also provide a sense of purpose and fulfillment.

In the pursuit of wealth, it becomes evident that relational and social wealth enriches our financial dimension by providing motivation, resilience, and opportunities for growth. It reinforces the idea that our individual financial success is intertwined with the well-being of our broader social network.

Balancing the Dimensions of Wealth

The interplay between these dimensions emphasizes the importance of striking a balance in our pursuit of wealth. An imbalance in any one dimension can lead to dissatisfaction, stress, or unfulfillment in our lives. For instance, an obsessive focus on financial wealth at the expense of mental and emotional well-being can result in burnout and a sense of emptiness.

Conversely, an overemphasis on mental and emotional well-being to the detriment of financial responsibility may lead to financial instability and insecurity. Neglecting relational and social wealth can result in isolation and a lack of support during challenging times.

The path to mastering the art of wealth requires us to nurture each dimension, recognizing that their harmonious interplay leads to a

24

life of true abundance and fulfillment. It invites us to set holistic goals that encompass financial success, emotional well-being, and meaningful relationships.

Ultimately, the journey to wealth mastery is not solely about accumulating riches but about cultivating a rich and meaningful life. It encourages us to align our financial choices, mental and emotional well-being, and relational and social connections with our values and aspirations. In doing so, we embark on a path that leads not only to financial security but also to a life of purpose, contentment, and lasting fulfillment. Our pursuit of holistic wealth reflects a profound shift in our perception of success—one that transcends the conventional notion of wealth as a solitary pursuit and redefines it as a holistic and harmonious journey. It beckons us to become stewards of our wealth, not merely collectors of possessions or achievements.

As we delve deeper into the chapters that follow, we will unravel the secrets of mastering the art of wealth in all its dimensions. We will explore the principles and practices that empower us to make sound financial decisions, cultivate emotional resilience, nurture enriching relationships, and leave a meaningful legacy. Together, we will navigate the complexities of wealth and discover that true abundance is not measured by the size of our bank accounts alone but by the depth of our experiences, the richness of our connections, and the positive impact we make in the world.

This journey is an invitation to transform your relationship with wealth and prosperity. It is an opportunity to embrace a life where financial success coexists harmoniously with mental and emotional well-being and where meaningful relationships provide a foundation for personal and collective growth. It is a call to action—to step onto the path of holistic wealth mastery and embark on a life-affirming voyage toward a future of genuine abundance, purpose, and fulfillment.

The Pursuit of Holistic Wealth

Our journey to wealth mastery begins with a fundamental shift in perspective—a recognition that wealth is not confined to a singular dimension of financial abundance but is a tapestry woven from the threads of financial success, mental and emotional well-being, and enriching relationships. This holistic understanding of wealth serves as our compass, guiding us toward a life of profound fulfillment and purpose.

Embracing the Multidimensional Nature of Wealth

To embark on the path of holistic wealth mastery, we must first embrace the concept of multidimensional wealth. It is an acknowledgment that our pursuit of riches extends beyond the accumulation of financial assets. While financial wealth is undoubtedly important, it is but one facet of the multifaceted gem that is wealth.

Imagine wealth as a three-dimensional sculpture, with each dimension representing a unique aspect of our lives:

1. **Financial Wealth:** This dimension encompasses our tangible assets, including savings, investments, properties, and income. It provides us with the means to meet our basic needs, plan for the future, and achieve financial goals.

2. **Mental and Emotional Wealth:** Here, we delve into the richness of our inner world, exploring the quality of our thoughts, emotions, and psychological well-being. A wealth of emotional intelligence, resilience, and a positive mindset enhances our overall quality of life.

3. **Relational and Social Wealth:** Relationships and social connections form the third dimension of wealth. These connections offer emotional support, create a sense of belonging, and provide opportunities for collaboration and personal growth.

In isolation, these dimensions offer glimpses of wealth, but their true magic unfolds when they intermingle and harmonize. The pursuit of holistic wealth is an invitation to balance these dimensions, recognizing that each influences and enriches the others. When we achieve this harmony, we unlock the door to true abundance—a wealth that transcends monetary measures and encompasses the entirety of our existence.

The Intersection of Dimensions: Where Fulfillment Flourishes

Picture a Venn diagram where the circles representing financial wealth, mental and emotional wealth, and relational and social wealth overlap. In the center, where all three circles converge, lies the space where fulfillment flourishes. This intersection represents a life of true wealth mastery—a life where financial success harmonizes with mental and emotional flourishing and enriching relationships.

Here, financial success is not pursued at the expense of well-being; instead, it is an integral part of a balanced and fulfilling life. A wealth of mental and emotional well-being empowers us to navigate financial challenges with grace and resilience. Enriching relationships provide the support and motivation needed to pursue financial goals while fostering a sense of belonging and purpose.

To illustrate the power of this intersection, consider the following scenarios:

- An individual achieves significant financial success but is burdened by stress and strained relationships. Despite their monetary wealth, they may find themselves lacking in fulfillment and overall well-being.

- Another person, while not necessarily affluent in monetary terms, enjoys a positive mindset, emotional resilience, and strong social connections. Their life is characterized by a sense of contentment, purpose, and meaningful relationships.

- Then, there's the individual who strikes a harmonious balance between financial prosperity, mental and emotional well-being, and enriching relationships. Their wealth extends beyond monetary measures, encompassing a fulfilling life marked by financial security, personal growth, and deep connections.

It is the last scenario that embodies the essence of holistic wealth mastery. It illustrates that true wealth is not confined to a singular dimension but is a dynamic interplay between financial, mental and emotional, and relational and social dimensions. This realization prompts us to embark on a transformative journey—one that empowers us to navigate life's complexities with wisdom, purpose, and a profound sense of fulfillment.

The Transformative Journey Toward Holistic Wealth Mastery

Our journey to holistic wealth mastery is an expedition into uncharted territory—a terrain where financial success is inextricably linked to mental and emotional well-being and enriching relationships. It is a voyage that demands self-reflection, intentionality, and the cultivation of a holistic approach to wealth.

As we navigate this transformative journey, we will explore the following key aspects:

1. **Balancing Act:** Discover the art of balancing the dimensions of wealth. Learn how to nurture your financial well-being without compromising your mental, emotional, or relational wealth. Understand that wealth is not a zero-sum game, and you can thrive in all dimensions simultaneously.

2. **Financial Wisdom:** Gain insights into responsible financial management, including budgeting, saving, investing, and debt management. Understand the principles of financial independence and wealth building that will empower you to achieve your financial aspirations.

3. **Emotional Resilience:** Cultivate emotional intelligence, resilience, and a positive mindset. Learn how to navigate life's challenges with grace and composure. Embrace adversity as an opportunity for growth and transformation.

4. **Relationship Enrichment:** Explore the art of building and nurturing meaningful relationships. Understand the importance of genuine connections, effective communication, and the reciprocity of social wealth. Learn how to create a network that supports your well-being and aspirations.

5. **Purposeful Living:** Discover the significance of aligning your financial choices, mental and emotional well-being, and relationships with your values and aspirations. Define your vision of a fulfilling life and set holistic goals that encompass all dimensions of wealth.

6. **The Legacy of Wealth:** Explore the idea of leaving a meaningful legacy that extends beyond financial assets. Understand the joy of giving back and the impact you can make through your wealth, whether it's through philanthropy, mentorship, or community engagement.

7. **Navigating Challenges:** Equip yourself with strategies for resilience and adaptability in the face of economic downturns, setbacks, and adversity. Learn from real-life stories of individuals who thrived despite formidable challenges.

8. **Ongoing Growth:** Embrace the notion that wealth mastery is an ongoing process, not a destination. Cultivate a mindset of continuous learning, growth, and adaptation as you navigate the ever-changing landscape of wealth.

Our journey to holistic wealth mastery is not without its challenges, but it is a journey that promises profound rewards. It is a journey that invites us to redefine success and wealth on our terms, to live with intention, and to savor the richness of a life well-lived.

As we embark on this transformative odyssey, we will explore each dimension of wealth in-depth, unveiling practical strategies and insights to empower you to master the art of wealth. Together, we will unlock the full potential of your financial success, mental and emotional well-being, and enriching relationships.

This book serves as your guide and companion on this journey—a journey that leads to a life of true abundance, purpose, and fulfillment. It is an exploration of holistic wealth, a tapestry woven from the threads of financial success, mental and emotional well-being, and enriching relationships. With each chapter, we will navigate the complexities of wealth mastery, equipping you with the tools and knowledge needed to craft a life that transcends monetary measures and embraces the full spectrum of human experience.

The pursuit of holistic wealth is not a destination but a continuous voyage—a voyage toward a life where financial success harmonizes with mental and emotional flourishing and enriching relationships. Together, we will uncover the path to true wealth mastery, where fulfillment becomes not just a distant dream but a living reality.

Chapter 2: Goal Setting and Financial Planning

Discussing the Significance of Setting Clear Financial Goals

Financial success is not a matter of chance or luck; it's the outcome of intentional planning and purposeful actions. At the core of this planning process is the art of setting clear and meaningful financial goals. In this chapter, we will embark on a profound exploration of why goal setting is an indispensable cornerstone on your journey to wealth mastery.

The Power of Purposeful Direction

Imagine a ship setting sail without a destination in mind, a journey marked by aimless drifting on the vast sea. Such a voyage, lacking purpose and direction, is unlikely to reach a meaningful destination or achieve any significant milestones. Similarly, in the realm of personal finance and wealth building, the absence of clear financial goals can leave us adrift, navigating life's financial waters without a concrete plan.

Financial goals act as the compass that provides direction to our financial journey. They are the lighthouses guiding us toward our desired destinations. Without them, we risk squandering our resources, missing opportunities, and feeling lost amidst the complexities of financial decisions.

Setting clear financial goals imbues our financial journey with purpose and intentionality. It defines what we aspire to achieve, both in the short term and long term, and empowers us to make informed choices that align with our objectives. In essence, financial goals are the foundation upon which we build our path to wealth mastery.

Defining Success on Your Terms

One of the remarkable aspects of setting financial goals is the ability to define success on your own terms. What constitutes financial success is a deeply personal and subjective matter, varying from one individual to another. For some, it may entail achieving financial independence and early retirement. For others, it might revolve around funding their children's education or traveling the world.

By establishing clear financial goals, you gain the autonomy to determine what success means to you. You are no longer bound by society's conventional definitions of wealth or success. Instead, you set your own benchmarks and milestones, creating a path that resonates with your values, aspirations, and unique circumstances.

This self-defined success becomes your North Star—a guiding light that illuminates your financial journey. It keeps you focused on what truly matters to you, allowing you to filter out distractions and prioritize actions that propel you toward your goals. This sense of purpose infuses your financial decisions with clarity and conviction.

The Motivating Force of Goals

Financial goals possess a remarkable capacity to serve as powerful motivators. They have the ability to ignite your ambition, inspire action, and fuel your determination. When you set clear and compelling goals, you create a vision of a brighter financial future—an image that propels you forward, even in the face of challenges.

Consider the difference between pursuing a vague notion of "saving money" versus working diligently toward a specific goal, such as "saving $10,000 for a down payment on a home." The latter goal provides a concrete target, a tangible objective that you can visualize and work toward. It fosters a sense of purpose and urgency, motivating you to allocate resources, manage expenses, and explore avenues for income growth.

Moreover, the achievement of financial goals is often accompanied by a sense of accomplishment and satisfaction. Each milestone reached reinforces your confidence and determination, encouraging you to set even loftier goals and push the boundaries of your financial capabilities. It's a virtuous cycle where success begets further success.

Enhancing Financial Decision-Making

One of the most significant advantages of setting clear financial goals is the enhanced decision-making process it facilitates. When you have a well-defined goal in mind, each financial decision becomes a stepping stone toward its realization.

Imagine you have set a goal to retire comfortably at the age of 55. With this objective in place, every financial choice you make—whether it's contributing to your retirement account, investing in assets with long-term growth potential, or reducing discretionary spending—becomes a deliberate action that aligns with your retirement goal.

This alignment of decisions with goals acts as a filter, helping you discern between what is essential and what is extraneous in your financial life. It encourages prudent financial behavior and discourages impulsive spending or choices that may derail your progress.

Furthermore, setting financial goals empowers you to make informed trade-offs. For instance, if your goal is to start your own business in five years, you may decide to allocate a portion of your income toward business development, which may require sacrifices in other areas of spending. The ability to make such trade-offs with a clear understanding of their impact on your goals is a hallmark of effective financial decision-making.

Measuring Progress and Celebrating Milestones

Financial goals provide a quantifiable framework for measuring your progress. They allow you to track your financial journey objectively, enabling you to assess how far you've come and how much closer you are to your goals.

Consider a goal to eliminate all high-interest debt within three years. As you make regular payments and reduce your outstanding balances, you can visually see your progress. Each debt paid off is a milestone achieved, signaling that you are one step closer to your goal of financial freedom.

The ability to measure progress in this manner offers several advantages:

1. **Motivation:** Seeing tangible progress reinforces your commitment to your goals. It reaffirms that your efforts are paying off and encourages you to persevere.

2. **Course Correction:** Measuring progress also allows you to identify any deviations from your plan early on. If you notice that you're falling behind, you can make necessary adjustments to get back on track.

3. **Celebration:** Achieving milestones gives you cause for celebration. It's an opportunity to acknowledge your hard work and dedication, fostering a sense of accomplishment and pride.

Types of Financial Goals

Financial goals come in various forms, each serving a specific purpose and time frame. Here are some common types of financial goals:

1. **Short-Term Goals:** These goals typically have a time frame of one to two years and focus on achieving immediate or near-future objectives. Examples include building an emergency fund, paying off credit card debt, or saving for a vacation. Short-term goals provide a sense of quick accomplishment and financial security.

2. **Mid-Term Goals:** Mid-term goals span from two to five years and often involve larger financial endeavors. Examples include saving for a down payment on a home, funding a child's education, or starting a business. These goals require consistent planning and discipline to reach significant milestones.

3. **Long-Term Goals:** Long-term goals extend beyond five years and encompass major life achievements. Examples include saving for retirement, achieving financial independence, or leaving a legacy for future generations. These goals necessitate careful planning, ongoing commitment, and strategic investment to secure a prosperous future.

4. **Specific Goals:** Specific goals are precisely defined and measurable. They answer the questions of what, why, and how much. For instance, a specific goal might be to save $20,000 for a new car within three years to enhance family mobility.

5. **Flexible Goals:** While setting clear goals is vital, it's also essential to allow room for flexibility. Life is unpredictable, and circumstances can change. Flexible goals can adapt to unexpected events while still keeping the overall financial direction intact.

6. **S.M.A.R.T. Goals:** A popular framework for setting financial goals is the S.M.A.R.T. criteria, which stands for

Specific, Measurable, Achievable, Relevant, and Time-Bound.
S.M.A.R.T. goals provide a structured approach to goal setting
that increases the likelihood of success.

7. **Bucket List Goals:** Some financial goals may not be
purely practical but rather emotionally fulfilling. These bucket list
goals include experiences like traveling to exotic destinations,
pursuing a passion project, or supporting a cause you're
passionate about.

8. **Family Goals:** Families often set collective financial goals,
such as saving for a family vacation, funding children's education,
or purchasing a family home. These goals strengthen family
bonds and shared aspirations.

9. **Career and Professional Goals:** Financial success is often
intertwined with professional growth. Goals related to career
advancement, income increases, or entrepreneurial ventures can
be instrumental in achieving financial well-being.

10. **Health and Wellness Goals:** Health and financial well-
being are interconnected. Goals related to improving physical and
mental health, such as investing in a fitness regimen or securing
health insurance, can contribute to long-term financial security.

The Psychology of Goal Setting

Goal setting is not merely a practical exercise; it also has a
profound psychological impact on our behavior and mindset.
When we set clear and meaningful goals, we activate a
psychological phenomenon known as the "goal-setting theory."
This theory posits that individuals who set specific and
challenging goals tend to perform better than those who do not.

Here's how goal setting influences our psychology:

1. **Motivation:** Goals provide motivation by creating a clear target to aim for. They give us a reason to act, especially when the goals are personally significant and compelling.

2. **Focus:** Setting goals narrows our focus, allowing us to concentrate our efforts and resources on what matters most. It helps us avoid distractions and stay on track.

3. **Persistence:** Goals encourage persistence in the face of setbacks and obstacles. When we encounter challenges, the desire to achieve our goals keeps us committed to finding solutions.

4. **Self-Confidence:** Accomplishing goals boosts self-confidence and self-efficacy, the belief in our ability to achieve future goals. Each success reinforces our belief in our capabilities.

5. **Accountability:** Goals provide a sense of accountability, both to ourselves and, in some cases, to others. This accountability can deter procrastination and increase commitment.

6. **Happiness and Well-Being:** Pursuing and achieving meaningful goals can lead to greater overall life satisfaction and well-being. It creates a sense of purpose and fulfillment.

The Process of Setting Financial Goals

Effective goal setting is a structured process that involves several key steps:

1. **Self-Reflection:** Begin by reflecting on your values, aspirations, and financial priorities. Consider what truly matters to you and what you want to achieve in different areas of your life.

2. **Prioritization:** Once you have a sense of your values and aspirations, prioritize your goals. Determine which goals are most important and urgent to you.

3. **Specificity:** Make your goals specific, measurable, and time-bound. Avoid vague or ambiguous goals. Instead, define what success looks like in clear, quantifiable terms.

4. **Breakdown:** Break down larger, long-term goals into smaller, manageable steps or milestones. This makes them less daunting and allows you to track progress more effectively.

5. **Plan:** Develop a plan for each goal that outlines the actions, resources, and timeline required for achievement. Consider potential obstacles and strategies to overcome them.

6. **Accountability:** Share your goals with a trusted friend, family member, or financial advisor who can provide support, encouragement, and accountability.

7. **Regular Review:** Regularly review your progress toward your goals. Adjust your plan as needed to stay on track and address changing circumstances.

The Power of Clear Financial Goals

Imagine embarking on a journey without a map or compass. The path ahead appears uncertain, filled with twists and turns, and the destination remains shrouded in ambiguity. Such a voyage, marked by confusion and aimlessness, is unlikely to yield a fulfilling and purpose-driven experience. Similarly, in the realm of personal finance and wealth building, the absence of clear financial goals can leave us adrift, navigating life's financial waters without a concrete plan. In this chapter, we will delve deep into the transformative power of setting clear financial goals—a compass that provides direction and purpose to your financial journey.

1. Clarity and Focus:

Setting clear financial goals brings a level of clarity and precision to your aspirations that mere wishes or vague desires cannot. It transforms abstract ideas about financial well-being into tangible, specific targets. When you know precisely what you're aiming for, you can concentrate your efforts, resources, and time with unwavering focus.

Imagine you have a goal to purchase your dream home in a specific neighborhood within five years. This goal gives your financial journey a clear destination. You're no longer merely "saving money" or "investing for the future"; you are working toward acquiring a specific property by a particular date. The clarity of your goal sharpens your financial decisions, influencing your choices about saving, investing, and spending.

Moreover, clear goals have a way of galvanizing your efforts. They become the guiding stars that illuminate your path, ensuring that you remain on course even in the midst of financial storms. When you face challenges or distractions, your defined goals serve as a constant reminder of what you're working toward. This laser-like focus on your objectives enhances your determination and resilience.

2. Motivation and Commitment:

Goals serve as potent motivators on your financial journey. They ignite the fire of determination within you, infusing your actions with purpose and drive. When you have a compelling reason to strive for financial success, you're more likely to stay committed to your goals, regardless of the obstacles that may arise.

40

Consider a goal to achieve financial independence by the age of
45. This goal is not merely a financial target; it represents the
opportunity to gain freedom and autonomy in your life. The
thought of breaking free from the constraints of traditional
employment and having the flexibility to pursue your passions
can be an incredibly motivating force.

Furthermore, clear financial goals provide a sense of
accountability. When you articulate your goals and share them
with a trusted friend, family member, or financial advisor, you
create a support system that holds you responsible for your
actions. This external accountability can be a powerful incentive
to stay on track and make consistent progress toward your goals.

3. Measurement and Progress Tracking:

Clear financial goals serve as measurable milestones along your
journey. They allow you to quantify your progress and assess
whether you're moving closer to your objectives. This
measurement is essential because it enables you to evaluate the
effectiveness of your financial strategies and make necessary
adjustments.

Imagine you've set a goal to accumulate $100,000 in a retirement
savings account within ten years. This goal provides a
quantifiable target. As you make regular contributions and
monitor your account's growth, you can objectively measure your
progress. If you find that you're falling behind, you can analyze
the reasons and take corrective actions, such as increasing your
contributions or exploring alternative investment strategies.

The ability to measure progress offers several advantages:

- **Motivation:** Seeing tangible progress reinforces your
commitment to your goals. It reaffirms that your efforts are
paying off and encourages you to persevere.

- **Course Correction:** Measuring progress allows you to identify any deviations from your plan early on. If you notice that you're falling behind, you can make necessary adjustments to get back on track.

- **Celebration:** Achieving milestones gives you cause for celebration. It's an opportunity to acknowledge your hard work and dedication, fostering a sense of accomplishment and pride.

4. Prioritization:

One of the most significant advantages of setting clear financial goals is their role in prioritizing your financial decisions. Goals act as filters, helping you discern between what is essential and what is extraneous in your financial life. They encourage prudent financial behavior by guiding your choices and discouraging impulsive spending or investments that may derail your progress.

Consider a goal to eliminate all high-interest debt within three years. With this goal in mind, you're more likely to prioritize debt repayment over discretionary spending on non-essential items. The alignment of your financial decisions with your goal ensures that your resources are allocated to actions that directly contribute to your objectives.

Furthermore, goals empower you to make informed trade-offs. If your goal is to start your own business in five years, you may decide to allocate a portion of your income toward business development. This allocation might require sacrifices in other areas of spending, such as dining out or entertainment. The ability to make such trade-offs with a clear understanding of their impact on your goals is a hallmark of effective financial decision-making.

5. Achievement and Satisfaction:

Ultimately, the pursuit and achievement of clear financial goals bring a profound sense of accomplishment and satisfaction. Each milestone reached becomes a testament to your financial competence and discipline. It is a tangible reminder of your ability to set objectives, plan effectively, and take action to achieve them.

Consider the satisfaction that comes with reaching a milestone like paying off a student loan or reaching a specific savings target for a major purchase. This achievement not only improves your financial position but also elevates your confidence in your ability to manage your financial affairs. It instills a sense of pride and self-assurance that can have a positive ripple effect on other areas of your life.

Furthermore, achieving financial goals often creates a positive feedback loop. The sense of accomplishment encourages you to set more ambitious goals and strive for even greater financial success. It reinforces the belief that you have control over your financial destiny and can shape your future according to your aspirations.

In essence, clear financial goals are not just waypoints on your journey; they are beacons of purpose and achievement. They provide direction, motivation, measurement, prioritization, and satisfaction, all of which contribute to your financial well-being and sense of fulfillment.

Types of Financial Goals

In the grand tapestry of financial planning, goals serve as the vibrant threads that weave together the intricate design of your financial life. These goals come in various forms, each with its own purpose, timeline, and significance. As you embark on your journey to wealth mastery, understanding the different types of financial goals is crucial. It empowers you to set clear objectives that align with your aspirations and life circumstances. Here, we explore the diverse landscape of financial goals, from the short-term to the long-term, and delve into the essence of lifestyle goals.

Short-Term Goals:

Short-term goals are the sprinters of the financial goal-setting world. They are the objectives you aim to achieve within a relatively brief timeframe, typically spanning one to two years. These goals are akin to quick wins that offer immediate or near-future rewards. Short-term goals play a pivotal role in providing a sense of accomplishment and financial security. They offer the satisfaction of rapid progress and tangible results.

Here are some common examples of short-term financial goals:

1. **Building an Emergency Fund:** Creating a financial safety net by saving three to six months' worth of living expenses. This goal provides a cushion for unexpected emergencies, such as medical expenses or car repairs.

2. **Paying Off High-Interest Debt:** Reducing and eliminating high-interest debt, such as credit card balances, payday loans, or personal loans. This goal not only relieves financial stress but also saves money on interest payments.

3. **Saving for a Vacation:** Setting aside funds for a well-deserved vacation or travel experience. This goal allows you to enjoy memorable experiences without resorting to debt.

4. **Buying a New Vehicle:** Accumulating a down payment for a new car or upgrading your current vehicle. This goal can enhance your mobility and transportation options.

5. **Home Repairs and Renovations:** Saving for necessary home improvements, repairs, or renovations. These projects can enhance your living space and property value.

Short-term goals are characterized by their immediacy and the need for focused, disciplined action. They provide a sense of financial stability and empower you to handle unexpected financial challenges confidently. Achieving short-term goals also reinforces the habit of goal setting and progress tracking, which are essential skills for long-term financial success.

Medium-Term Goals:

Medium-term goals are the middle-distance runners of the financial goal-setting journey. They typically extend from two to five years and often involve more substantial financial endeavors. These goals bridge the gap between immediate needs and long-term aspirations, requiring consistent planning and discipline.

Examples of medium-term financial goals include:

1. **Saving for a Down Payment:** Accumulating funds for a down payment on a home or other significant purchase. This goal sets the stage for homeownership and long-term financial stability.

2. **Funding Education:** Saving for a child's education or your own ongoing education and professional development. This goal ensures access to quality education without the burden of excessive student loans.

3. **Starting a Business:** Capitalizing on an entrepreneurial vision by saving for startup costs or initial investments. This goal fuels your entrepreneurial journey and financial independence.

4. **Building an Investment Portfolio:** Establishing and growing an investment portfolio with the aim of generating passive income or wealth accumulation. This goal aligns with long-term wealth-building strategies.

Medium-term goals require careful planning and commitment. They often involve larger financial commitments and may necessitate adjustments to your budget and savings strategy. Achieving these goals offers a sense of progress toward significant life milestones.

Long-Term Goals:

Long-term goals are the marathon runners of the financial goal-setting landscape. They extend beyond five years and encompass major life achievements and financial milestones. Long-term goals shape your financial destiny, influencing your lifestyle in retirement, your legacy for future generations, and your overall financial security.

Examples of long-term financial goals include:

1. **Retirement Planning:** Saving and investing for a comfortable and financially secure retirement. This goal involves building a nest egg that can sustain your desired lifestyle after retirement.

2. **Financial Independence:** Achieving financial independence, which means having sufficient passive income to cover your living expenses without relying on traditional employment. This goal grants you the freedom to pursue your passions and interests.

3. **Legacy Building:** Planning for the transfer of wealth to future generations or philanthropic endeavors. This goal allows

you to leave a lasting impact on your family, community, or causes you care deeply about.

4. **Real Estate Investments:** Acquiring and managing income-producing properties or real estate investments. This goal can provide ongoing rental income and long-term wealth growth.

5. **Business Succession:** Preparing for the transition or sale of a business you own. This goal ensures a smooth handover and maximizes the value of your entrepreneurial endeavors.

Long-term goals require a strategic approach that includes diligent saving, investing, and risk management. They are a testament to your vision for the future and your commitment to long-term financial well-being. Achieving long-term goals often involves multiple intermediate steps and may evolve over time as your circumstances change.

Lifestyle Goals:

While many financial goals are practical and financially oriented, lifestyle goals add a layer of personal fulfillment and well-being to your financial journey. These goals encompass choices about your housing, travel, leisure, and other personal preferences. Lifestyle goals contribute to your overall sense of happiness, contentment, and quality of life.

Examples of lifestyle goals include:

1. **Homeownership:** Achieving the dream of homeownership by purchasing a house or property that aligns with your desired lifestyle and location.

2. **Travel and Adventure:** Planning and embarking on travel adventures to explore new cultures, destinations, and experiences.

3. **Leisure and Hobbies:** Budgeting for hobbies, interests, and leisure activities that bring joy and fulfillment to your life, whether it's a golf membership, art classes, or a musical instrument.

4. **Health and Wellness:** Investing in your physical and mental well-being through fitness memberships, wellness retreats, or health-related experiences.

5. **Charitable Giving:** Incorporating charitable giving into your financial plan to support causes and organizations that resonate with your values and beliefs.

Lifestyle goals celebrate the joy of living life to the fullest and creating a life that reflects your passions and interests. While they may not have a specific financial target, they enrich your life in meaningful ways.

Setting SMART Financial Goals

The journey to wealth mastery begins with a vision—a clear and compelling picture of what you want your financial future to look like. This vision, however, is not enough on its own. To turn your aspirations into reality, you need a roadmap, a set of well-structured financial goals that will guide your actions, keep you on track, and measure your progress along the way. Enter the SMART framework—a powerful tool that transforms vague desires into actionable and achievable objectives.

Specific: Defining the What, Where, and How

The first letter in SMART stands for "Specific." Your financial goals should be precisely defined, leaving no room for ambiguity or misinterpretation. They answer the fundamental questions of what, where, and how.

When setting specific financial goals, consider the following:

1. **What:** Clearly state what you want to achieve. Be specific about the outcome you desire. For example, instead of a vague goal like "save money," a specific goal would be "save $10,000 for a down payment on a home."

2. **Where:** If your goal involves a specific location or context, include that information. For instance, if your goal relates to purchasing a property, specify the location or type of property you have in mind.

3. **How:** Describe how you plan to achieve the goal. Outline the steps, strategies, or actions you will take to make it happen. This transforms your goal from a mere wish into a concrete plan.

A specific financial goal provides clarity and focus, ensuring that you know exactly what you're working toward. It eliminates confusion and sets a clear direction for your financial journey. Specificity allows you to break down larger objectives into manageable tasks, making them more achievable.

Measurable: Quantifying Progress and Success

The "M" in SMART represents "Measurable." Measurable goals are those that you can quantify and track. They provide a clear way to measure your progress and determine whether you've successfully achieved the goal.

To make your financial goals measurable, consider the following:

1. **Quantify:** Express your goal in specific numbers, such as dollars, percentages, or units. This allows you to track your progress objectively. For example, instead of saying "pay off debt," make it measurable by stating, "pay off $5,000 in credit card debt."

49

2. **Set Milestones:** Break down larger goals into smaller milestones or checkpoints. These interim targets serve as indicators of progress and motivation. For instance, if your long-term goal is to save $100,000 for retirement, set measurable milestones along the way, such as saving $10,000 each year.

3. **Define Success:** Determine what success looks like for each goal. Clearly establish the criteria for achievement. This eliminates subjectivity and ensures that you can definitively say whether you've reached the goal.

Measurable financial goals enable you to track your journey effectively. They provide a sense of direction and allow you to assess whether you're making the necessary progress. This tracking mechanism also helps you stay accountable and make adjustments if you're falling behind.

Achievable: Realistic and Attainable Goals

The "A" in SMART stands for "Achievable." Achievable goals are those that are realistic and attainable within your current financial situation and available resources.

To ensure your financial goals are achievable, consider the following:

1. **Assess Resources:** Evaluate your current financial resources, including income, savings, and investments. Determine whether you have the means to pursue the goal or whether additional resources are required.

2. **Consider Constraints:** Take into account any constraints or limitations that might impact your ability to achieve the goal. Consider factors such as time, budget, and external circumstances.

3. **Set Realistic Expectations:** Be realistic about the timeframe and effort required to achieve the goal. Avoid setting overly ambitious goals that may lead to frustration or burnout.

4. **Prioritize:** If you have multiple financial goals, prioritize them based on importance and feasibility. Focus on one goal at a time to increase your chances of success.

Achievable financial goals strike a balance between ambition and realism. They challenge you to stretch your capabilities while acknowledging the constraints and limitations you may face. By setting attainable goals, you enhance your confidence and motivation, increasing the likelihood of successful achievement.

Relevant: Goals Aligned with Values and Vision

The "R" in SMART represents "Relevant." Relevant goals are those that align with your values, priorities, and long-term vision. They are meaningful and relevant to your life.

To ensure your financial goals are relevant, consider the following:

1. **Alignment with Values:** Reflect on whether the goal aligns with your core values and beliefs. Does it contribute to your overall sense of purpose and fulfillment?

2. **Long-Term Vision:** Assess how the goal fits into your long-term vision for your financial future. Will achieving this goal bring you closer to your desired lifestyle and aspirations?

3. **Immediate Impact:** Consider whether the goal has immediate or long-term benefits. Does it address a pressing financial need or contribute to your long-term financial well-being?

4. **Personal Motivation:** Reflect on your personal motivation and commitment to the goal. Are you genuinely enthusiastic about pursuing it, or is it driven by external pressures or expectations?

Relevant financial goals resonate with your values and aspirations, creating a sense of purpose and meaning. They inspire intrinsic motivation and enthusiasm, making it more likely that you will stay dedicated to achieving them. When your goals are relevant, they become integral to your larger financial plan and vision.

Time-Bound: Adding Urgency and Accountability

The final letter in SMART is "T," which stands for "Time-Bound." Time-bound goals have a defined timeframe or deadline attached to them. This element introduces a sense of urgency and accountability.

To make your financial goals time-bound, consider the following:

1. **Specify a Deadline:** Determine when you want to achieve the goal. Attach a specific date or timeframe to provide clarity about the timeline. For example, instead of saying "save for retirement," state, "save $500,000 for retirement by age 60."

2. **Set Milestones:** If the goal spans several years, establish interim milestones with corresponding deadlines. This ensures that you're making consistent progress toward the ultimate goal.

3. **Regular Review:** Schedule regular reviews to assess your progress and make any necessary adjustments. This ongoing evaluation helps you stay on track and meet your deadlines.

Time-bound financial goals create a sense of urgency, preventing procrastination and complacency. They serve as a built-in accountability mechanism, pushing you to take consistent action toward achieving the goal. Deadlines also enable you to prioritize your financial objectives effectively.

Incorporating the SMART framework into your goal-setting process transforms your financial aspirations into tangible and achievable objectives. It guides you through the process of defining clear, measurable, achievable, relevant, and time-bound goals. With SMART goals in place, you have a roadmap that enhances clarity, motivation, accountability, and success on your journey to wealth mastery.

Provide Strategies for Effective Financial Planning

Effective financial planning is the cornerstone of building wealth and achieving financial success. It serves as the bridge that connects your financial goals with actionable steps, transforming your aspirations into a tangible roadmap for success. In this chapter, we will explore a range of strategies to help you craft an effective financial plan that aligns with your goals and aspirations.

1. Assess Your Current Financial Situation

Before you can chart a course toward financial success, you must first understand where you currently stand. This begins with a comprehensive assessment of your financial situation. Here's how to get started:

   - **Calculate Your Net Worth:** Determine your net worth by subtracting your liabilities (debts) from your assets. This figure provides a snapshot of your overall financial health.

- **Analyze Income and Expenses:** Take a close look at your income sources and expenses. Understanding your cash flow is crucial for effective financial planning.

- **Review Existing Assets and Liabilities:** Assess your existing assets, such as savings accounts, investments, and real estate holdings. Additionally, review any outstanding debts or loans.

A clear understanding of your current financial situation provides a solid foundation upon which you can build your financial plan.

2. Define Your Financial Goals

With a firm grasp of your current financial status, the next step is to define your financial goals. These goals serve as the driving force behind your financial plan and provide direction for your actions. Consider the following:

- **Short-Term Goals:** These are objectives you aim to achieve within a year or less. They may include building an emergency fund, paying off high-interest debt, or saving for a vacation.

- **Medium-Term Goals:** Medium-term goals typically span one to five years and may include saving for a down payment on a home, funding a child's education, or starting a small business.

- **Long-Term Goals:** Long-term goals extend beyond five years and often involve major life events such as retirement planning, building a substantial investment portfolio, or leaving a financial legacy.

Ensure that your financial goals are SMART (Specific, Measurable, Achievable, Relevant, and Time-Bound). SMART goals provide clarity and focus, making it easier to develop a plan to achieve them.

3. Create a Budget

A well-structured budget is a foundational tool for effective financial planning. It allows you to allocate your income in a way that aligns with your goals and priorities. Here's how to create a budget:

  - **Income Analysis:** Begin by listing all sources of income, including your salary, investments, rental income, and any other revenue streams.

  - **Expense Tracking:** Carefully track your monthly expenses, categorizing them into essentials (such as housing, utilities, and groceries) and discretionary spending (such as entertainment and dining out).

  - **Set Spending Limits:** Establish spending limits for each category based on your financial goals. Ensure that your budget allocates a portion of your income to savings and investments.

  - **Regular Review:** Periodically review your budget to ensure that you are adhering to your spending limits and making progress toward your financial goals. Adjust your budget as needed.

A well-crafted budget empowers you to manage your finances effectively, prioritize your goals, and track your progress.

4. Build an Emergency Fund

An emergency fund is your financial safety net, providing peace of mind and protection against unexpected expenses or disruptions to your income. Aim to set aside three to six months' worth of living expenses in a readily accessible account. This fund acts as a financial cushion in case of job loss, medical emergencies, or unforeseen expenses.

5. Pay Off High-Interest Debt

High-interest debt, such as credit card balances, can be a significant obstacle to wealth building. Prioritize paying off high-interest debt as part of your financial plan. Allocate extra funds toward debt repayment while making minimum payments on lower-interest debts. Reducing and eventually eliminating high-interest debt frees up more of your income for savings and investments.

6. Develop an Investment Strategy

Investing is a powerful wealth-building tool that can help your money grow over time. To develop an effective investment strategy:

   - **Determine Risk Tolerance:** Assess your risk tolerance by considering your comfort level with investment fluctuations. Your risk tolerance will influence your investment choices.

   - **Set Investment Goals:** Define your investment goals, such as retirement planning, funding education, or wealth accumulation. Each goal may have a different investment timeline and risk profile.

   - **Create a Diversified Portfolio:** Build a diversified investment portfolio that aligns with your risk tolerance and goals. Diversification reduces risk by spreading investments across different asset classes, such as stocks, bonds, and real estate.

  - **Regularly Monitor and Rebalance:** Keep a close eye on your investments and make adjustments as needed to maintain your desired asset allocation. Regular monitoring ensures that your portfolio aligns with your goals.

7. Review and Adjust

Financial planning is not a one-time event but an ongoing process. Life circumstances, market conditions, and personal goals can change over time, necessitating revisions to your financial plan. Regularly review your plan and make adjustments as needed. This ongoing evaluation ensures that your financial plan remains relevant and effective in helping you achieve your goals.

Effective financial planning is the key to turning your financial goals into reality. By assessing your current financial situation, defining clear goals, creating a budget, building an emergency fund, paying off high-interest debt, developing an investment strategy, and regularly reviewing and adjusting your plan, you can create a robust roadmap to financial success. In the chapters that follow, we will delve deeper into each of these strategies, providing you with the tools and insights you need to craft an effective financial plan that aligns with your unique goals and aspirations.

Examples of Successful Individuals

Throughout history and in contemporary times, there are numerous individuals who have demonstrated the transformative power of goal setting and effective financial planning. Their stories serve as inspirational examples of what can be achieved through clear objectives and disciplined execution. These individuals have not only achieved financial success but have also made a lasting impact on their respective fields and beyond. Let's explore some of these remarkable individuals:

1. Warren Buffett: The Oracle of Omaha

Warren Buffett, often referred to as the Oracle of Omaha, is one of the world's most successful investors. His disciplined approach to investing and wealth accumulation has made him a household name. What sets Buffett apart is his ability to set clear investment goals and stick to his strategy with unwavering determination.

Buffett's journey to wealth began with a clear objective: to become a successful investor. He started by saving and investing at a young age and developed a value-oriented approach to stock investing. One of his most famous goals was to become a millionaire by the time he turned 35, a goal he achieved and surpassed. His long-term investment horizon and focus on acquiring undervalued companies have made him one of the wealthiest individuals globally.

2. Oprah Winfrey: From Challenging Upbringing to Media Mogul

Oprah Winfrey's life story is a testament to the power of setting and pursuing ambitious goals. Born into a challenging upbringing, Oprah faced numerous obstacles on her path to success. However, her ability to leverage her talents and aspirations allowed her to overcome adversity and build an empire.

Oprah set a series of career and personal goals that guided her journey. From becoming a successful radio host to launching her talk show, "The Oprah Winfrey Show," she continuously aimed higher and achieved her objectives. Her ability to connect with audiences and her unwavering commitment to personal growth propelled her to media stardom. Oprah serves as an inspiration not only for her financial success but also for her dedication to philanthropy and making a positive impact on the world.

3. Elon Musk: Visionary Entrepreneur

Elon Musk is a visionary entrepreneur known for his audacious goals and relentless pursuit of innovation. His ambitious objectives include revolutionizing space travel through SpaceX, transitioning the world to sustainable energy with Tesla, and creating a high-speed transportation system with the Hyperloop.

Musk's goals extend far beyond financial success; they encompass reshaping industries and advancing humanity's future. His determination to achieve these goals is evident in his tireless work ethic and willingness to take on immense challenges. Musk's ventures have redefined the boundaries of what is possible and serve as a testament to the impact of setting visionary objectives.

4. "The Millionaire Next Door": Lessons from Everyday Millionaires

While individual success stories like those of Warren Buffett, Oprah Winfrey, and Elon Musk are awe-inspiring, there are valuable lessons to be learned from everyday millionaires as well. "The Millionaire Next Door," a book by Dr. Thomas J. Stanley and Dr. William D. Danko, provides insights into the habits and behaviors of self-made millionaires.

The authors conducted extensive research on millionaires and discovered that many achieved wealth through diligent savings, frugal living, and smart investment choices. These millionaires often set clear financial goals, such as saving a certain percentage of their income or reaching a specific net worth milestone. They prioritized long-term financial security over short-term consumption, demonstrating the power of disciplined financial planning.

These examples illustrate that achieving financial success is not limited to a select few but is attainable through clear goals, disciplined execution, and a commitment to personal growth. Whether it's through value investing like Warren Buffett, media entrepreneurship like Oprah Winfrey, visionary innovation like Elon Musk, or prudent financial management like the millionaires next door, these individuals showcase the diverse paths to wealth and the transformative impact of setting and pursuing meaningful objectives.

Empowerment Through Goals and Planning

Goal setting and financial planning are not mere exercises in number crunching; they are powerful tools that empower you to take control of your financial future. By setting clear and meaningful financial goals and crafting an effective plan to achieve them, you embark on a journey toward financial success and holistic well-being. In the chapters that follow, we will delve deeper into the strategies and insights that will help you translate your financial aspirations into reality

Chapter 3: The Wealth Mindset

Exploring the Mindset and Attitudes that Contribute to Wealth Creation

When it comes to building wealth, it's not just about numbers and financial strategies; it's also about the mindset and attitudes that shape your financial decisions. In this chapter, we will delve into the essential components of a wealth mindset, examine common mental barriers that hinder financial success, and draw inspiration from real-life stories of individuals who transformed their mindset to achieve financial prosperity.

The Wealth Mindset Unveiled

In the world of wealth-building, the mindset and attitudes individuals hold toward financial success can be the differentiating factors between thriving and struggling. Imagine two individuals with similar financial backgrounds and opportunities, yet one attains financial success while the other constantly struggles to make ends meet. What sets them apart? It's often their mindset and attitudes toward wealth.

1. Abundance Mentality: Seeing Opportunity Everywhere

Individuals with a wealth mindset possess what is commonly referred to as an "abundance mentality." This mentality is characterized by a belief in the abundant nature of opportunities and resources. Those with an abundance mentality perceive the world as brimming with possibilities for financial growth, and they reject the notion that success is a finite resource reserved for a lucky few.

The abundance mentality empowers individuals to see potential where others might perceive limitations. Instead of dwelling on scarcity or dwelling on what they lack, those with this mindset focus on what they can create and achieve. They understand that the world is not a zero-sum game, and by creating value for themselves and others, they can tap into a wealth of opportunities.

2. Goal Orientation: Setting Clear Objectives

A wealth mindset is inherently goal-oriented. It involves the practice of setting clear and meaningful financial objectives and working diligently to achieve them. These goals act as guiding stars, providing direction and purpose on the journey to wealth mastery.

Individuals with a wealth mindset understand that wealth doesn't materialize overnight. It's the result of consistent effort and persistence over time. They don't view financial success as an abstract concept but as a tangible destination they are actively striving to reach. By defining their goals and breaking them down into actionable steps, they ensure that their financial decisions are purpose-driven and aligned with their objectives.

3. Financial Literacy: Valuing Knowledge and Education

A wealth mindset places a high value on financial literacy and continuous learning. It recognizes the importance of understanding financial principles, concepts, and strategies. Those with this mindset actively seek out opportunities to enhance their financial knowledge and make informed decisions.

Financial literacy is the foundation upon which individuals with a wealth mindset build their financial success. It empowers them to navigate complex financial landscapes, make informed investment choices, and protect their assets. They understand that education is an ongoing process, and they are committed to staying informed about the ever-evolving world of finance.

4. Risk Management: Calculated and Thoughtful Risk-Taking

Individuals with a wealth mindset are not averse to risk, but they approach it thoughtfully and strategically. They understand that calculated risks can lead to opportunities for growth and wealth creation. Rather than shying away from risk, they embrace it as an integral part of the wealth-building process.

This approach to risk management involves careful assessment and evaluation of potential risks and rewards. Those with a wealth mindset engage in thorough research and due diligence before making investment decisions. They diversify their investment portfolios to spread risk and minimize exposure to any single asset class. By understanding the interplay of risk and reward, they make informed choices that align with their financial goals.

5. Delayed Gratification: Prioritizing Long-Term Gain

Patience is a hallmark of the wealth mindset. It involves the ability to delay immediate desires and instant gratification for the sake of long-term gain. This mindset recognizes that building wealth is not a sprint but a marathon, requiring discipline and sacrifice along the way.

Individuals with a wealth mindset prioritize saving and investing over impulsive spending. They understand that accumulating wealth requires making choices that may not yield immediate rewards but will contribute to their financial security and well-being in the future. Delayed gratification empowers them to make decisions that align with their long-term goals rather than succumbing to the allure of short-term pleasures.

The wealth mindset is a powerful force that can propel individuals toward financial success and holistic well-being. It is characterized by an abundance mentality, goal orientation, a commitment to financial literacy, thoughtful risk management, and the ability to practice delayed gratification. This mindset empowers individuals to navigate the complexities of wealth-building with confidence and purpose, ensuring that their financial decisions align with their values and aspirations. As we continue our journey toward wealth mastery in the chapters that follow, we will delve deeper into these mindset principles and explore practical strategies for cultivating and harnessing the wealth mindset in your own life.

Overcoming Mental Barriers to Financial Success

In our pursuit of wealth mastery, we often encounter mental barriers that can impede our progress. These barriers are deeply ingrained beliefs and attitudes that limit our financial potential and hinder the cultivation of a wealth mindset. However, with self-awareness and the right strategies, we can overcome these barriers and unlock our full financial potential. In this chapter, we will explore some common mental barriers and effective strategies to overcome them.

1. Scarcity Mentality: Shifting from Lack to Abundance

One of the most pervasive mental barriers to financial success is the scarcity mentality. This mindset is rooted in the belief that there is never enough—never enough money, never enough resources, never enough opportunities. It breeds fear and anxiety about money and can lead to destructive financial behaviors.

Overcoming the scarcity mentality requires a fundamental shift in perspective. Instead of focusing on what you lack, cultivate an abundance mentality. Recognize that the world is full of opportunities and resources waiting to be tapped. Practice gratitude by acknowledging the abundance that already exists in your life. Mindfulness can also help change your perspective, allowing you to appreciate the present moment and the possibilities it holds.

2. Fear of Failure: Embracing Setbacks as Learning Opportunities

The fear of failure is another mental barrier that can paralyze financial decision-making. Many individuals avoid taking risks or pursuing opportunities because they are afraid of failing. However, failure is an inherent part of any journey to success, and it often provides valuable lessons.

To overcome the fear of failure, reframe your perception of it. Instead of viewing failure as a final outcome, see it as a stepping stone toward success. Each setback is an opportunity to learn, grow, and improve. Embrace a growth mindset, which is the belief that your abilities and intelligence can be developed through effort and learning. By maintaining this perspective, you'll be more willing to take calculated risks and persevere in the face of adversity.

3. Self-Doubt: Challenging Self-Limiting Beliefs

Self-doubt can erode confidence in your financial abilities and limit your potential for success. It often manifests as self-limiting beliefs—negative thoughts and assumptions about your capabilities. These beliefs can become self-fulfilling prophecies, preventing you from taking necessary actions to improve your financial situation.

65

To overcome self-doubt, challenge these self-limiting beliefs. Seek knowledge and education to build your financial confidence. Set achievable financial goals and celebrate your successes, no matter how small they may seem. Surround yourself with a supportive network of friends, family, or mentors who believe in your abilities and can provide encouragement and guidance.

4. Procrastination: Breaking Down Financial Tasks

Procrastination is a common barrier to financial success, especially when it comes to tasks like saving, investing, and financial planning. Delaying these crucial actions can hinder your progress and prevent you from reaching your financial goals.

To overcome procrastination, break down financial tasks into smaller, more manageable steps. Instead of trying to tackle your entire financial plan at once, focus on one aspect at a time. Establish routines and habits that make financial tasks a regular part of your life. For example, designate a specific time each month to review your budget and investment portfolio. By taking incremental steps and creating routines, you can overcome the inertia of procrastination and make steady progress toward your financial objectives.

5. Impulse Spending: Practicing Mindful Financial Behavior

Impulse spending is a behavior that can sabotage your financial goals. It involves making unplanned and often unnecessary purchases that can drain your financial resources.

To combat impulse spending, create a budget that outlines your financial priorities and limits discretionary spending. Set clear spending limits for categories like dining out, entertainment, and shopping. Before making a purchase, pause and ask yourself whether it aligns with your financial goals and values. Practicing mindful spending can help you become more aware of your financial choices and curb impulsive behavior.

Personal Stories of Transformation

The journey from mental barriers to a wealth mindset is a powerful one, marked by personal determination and resilience. Let's draw inspiration from real-life stories of individuals who overcame these barriers to achieve financial success:

1. Sarah's Transformation from Scarcity to Abundance

Sarah grew up in a household where money was always a source of stress and anxiety. As a result, she developed a scarcity mentality, constantly worrying about financial security. However, as an adult, Sarah recognized the negative impact this mindset was having on her life.

To overcome her scarcity mentality, Sarah started practicing gratitude daily. She began journaling about the things she was thankful for, no matter how small. Over time, she shifted her focus from what she lacked to the abundance of blessings in her life. This change in perspective not only reduced her financial anxiety but also empowered her to take control of her finances and make more informed decisions.

2. Mark's Journey from Fear to Resilience

Mark had always been afraid of taking financial risks. He avoided investing in the stock market and missed out on potential opportunities for wealth accumulation. However, he realized that his fear of failure was holding him back from achieving his financial goals.

Mark decided to embrace the idea that failure is a part of the learning process. He started by investing a small amount in stocks

and educated himself about investment strategies. While he faced
setbacks along the way, he viewed each loss as a valuable lesson.
Over time, Mark developed resilience and a greater willingness to
take calculated risks. His investment portfolio grew, and he
achieved financial milestones he had once thought were
unattainable.

3. Lisa's Transformation from Self-Doubt to Confidence

Lisa had always struggled with self-doubt when it came to her
career and finances. She believed that she lacked the skills and
knowledge needed to manage her finances effectively. However,
she decided to challenge these self-limiting beliefs.

Lisa enrolled in financial literacy courses and sought guidance
from a financial advisor. As she gained knowledge and skills, her
confidence grew. She set achievable financial goals and
celebrated each accomplishment along the way. Surrounding
herself with a supportive network of friends and mentors further
boosted her confidence. Lisa's journey from self-doubt to
financial confidence not only improved her financial situation but
also empowered her to make informed decisions and take control
of her financial future.

4. John's Progress from Procrastination to Discipline

John had always struggled with procrastination when it came to
his finances. He would put off important financial tasks, such as
creating a budget or reviewing his investment portfolio, until the
last minute. This habit often led to missed opportunities and
financial stress.

To overcome his procrastination tendencies, John adopted a
systematic approach to financial planning. He broke down his
financial goals into smaller, manageable steps and created a
calendar with specific deadlines for each task. By establishing

routines and making financial responsibilities a regular part of his life, John gradually built discipline.

As he saw progress and positive changes in his financial situation, John's motivation grew. He began to view financial tasks as opportunities rather than burdens. His disciplined approach allowed him to stay on track with his financial goals, and he achieved milestones that once seemed elusive.

5. Emily's Journey from Impulse Spending to Mindful Budgeting

Emily had a penchant for impulse spending, particularly on items she didn't truly need. Her financial statements were filled with impulsive purchases that left her with little savings and mounting credit card debt.

To combat this habit, Emily created a detailed budget that outlined her financial priorities. She set clear spending limits for discretionary categories and used cash envelopes to control her spending. Before making a purchase, she would pause and ask herself whether it aligned with her financial goals and values. This practice of mindful spending made her more conscious of her financial choices.

Over time, Emily's budgeting and mindful spending habits paid off. She saw a significant reduction in her credit card debt, and her savings began to grow. Emily learned that by making intentional financial decisions, she could achieve her goals and enjoy a more secure financial future.

These personal stories illustrate that while mental barriers can be formidable, they are not insurmountable. With determination, self-awareness, and the right strategies, individuals can transform their mindset and behaviors to achieve financial success. The journey from scarcity to abundance, fear to resilience, self-doubt to confidence, procrastination to discipline, and impulse spending to mindful budgeting is a testament to the power of the human spirit and the potential for positive change.

Case Study 1: Sarah's Journey from Debt to Financial Freedom

Sarah's story is a testament to the transformative power of financial education and disciplined financial management. Not too long ago, Sarah found herself trapped in a cycle of debt, burdened by credit card balances and living paycheck to paycheck. The weight of her financial obligations was taking a toll on her mental and emotional well-being.

Sarah's turning point came when she recognized the need for change. She decided to take control of her financial future by seeking out resources and knowledge. She began her journey toward financial freedom by enrolling in financial literacy courses, reading books on personal finance, and attending seminars.

One of the key principles Sarah learned early on was the importance of budgeting. She created a detailed budget that outlined her income, expenses, and debt repayment plan. Sarah made a commitment to reduce her discretionary spending and direct those funds toward paying off her high-interest credit card debt.

As she diligently followed her budget and chipped away at her debt, Sarah began to see progress. Small victories, such as paying off her first credit card, provided motivation to keep going. She celebrated each milestone, no matter how minor, which kept her focused and encouraged.

To accelerate her journey to financial freedom, Sarah also explored additional income streams. She took on freelance work in her spare time and invested in her skills to increase her earning potential. The extra income allowed her to pay off her debts faster and build an emergency fund for future financial security.

Once Sarah had eliminated her credit card debt, she shifted her focus to long-term financial planning. She began investing in stocks and bonds, following a conservative investment strategy that aligned with her risk tolerance and goals. Over time, her investments grew, providing her with a sense of financial stability and the potential for future wealth accumulation.

Today, Sarah is not only debt-free but also well on her way to financial independence. Her story serves as an inspiration to others who find themselves trapped in the cycle of debt, showing that with determination, education, and disciplined financial management, it is possible to break free and build a more secure financial future.

Case Study 2: John's Resilience and Reinvention

John's financial journey was marked by several setbacks that could have discouraged even the most determined individuals. He faced the challenges of a failed business venture and job loss, which left him financially strained and uncertain about his future.

However, John refused to be defined by his setbacks. Instead, he viewed these challenges as opportunities for growth and reinvention. He recognized that his financial well-being was not solely determined by external circumstances but also by his mindset and actions.

John's first step toward recovery was to assess his skills and identify new opportunities. He invested in further education and training, acquiring skills that were in demand in the job market. While it was a challenging period, John remained committed to his vision of financial stability.

During his job search, John discovered the world of consulting and freelancing. He recognized that these fields offered flexibility and the potential for increased income. With determination, he launched his own consulting business, leveraging his expertise and network to secure clients.

As his consulting business began to thrive, John turned his attention to building a diversified income portfolio. He explored different investment opportunities, including stocks, real estate, and peer-to-peer lending. Through careful research and risk management, he gradually increased his investments, creating multiple income streams.

John's story highlights the importance of resilience and adaptability in the face of financial setbacks. His ability to pivot his career, embrace new opportunities, and build a robust financial foundation serves as a testament to the transformative power of determination and continuous learning.

Case Study 3: Maria's Shift to an Abundance Mindset

Maria's journey is a remarkable example of how a shift in mindset can lead to profound changes in one's financial life and the lives of others. Growing up in a family that struggled financially, Maria was accustomed to a scarcity mindset, which instilled a sense of limitation and fear when it came to money.

However, Maria refused to accept this limited perspective. She embarked on a personal development journey that included mindset training, self-reflection, and the exploration of abundance principles. Through this process, she gradually transformed her mindset from one of scarcity to one of abundance.

One of the key principles Maria embraced was the belief that there is an abundance of opportunities and resources in the world.

She recognized that by changing her beliefs and attitudes toward wealth, she could change her financial reality.

With her newfound abundance mindset, Maria took bold steps to create financial prosperity for herself and her community. She decided to start a business that aligned with her passions and skills. She invested time and effort into developing her entrepreneurial abilities and soon launched a successful venture.

As her business flourished, Maria's income grew substantially. Instead of hoarding her newfound wealth, she chose to share it generously with her community. She supported local charities, educational programs, and initiatives that aimed to uplift those in need.

Maria's story exemplifies the profound impact that a shift in mindset can have on one's financial success and overall well-being. Her journey from scarcity to abundance not only transformed her own life but also allowed her to make a meaningful and positive impact on the lives of others.

These case studies illustrate the diversity of paths that individuals can take on their journey to wealth mastery. Whether it's overcoming debt, turning setbacks into opportunities, or shifting from a scarcity mindset to an abundance mindset, each story showcases the potential for personal and financial growth. In the following chapters, we will explore the strategies and principles that can help you navigate your unique path toward financial success and holistic well-being.

Nurturing Your Wealth Mindset**

The wealth mindset is not a fixed state; it's a dynamic quality that can be cultivated and nurtured. As you embark on your own journey to financial success, remember that your mindset is a powerful tool. It shapes your beliefs, drives your actions, and ultimately determines your financial outcomes. By exploring the components of a wealth mindset, acknowledging and overcoming mental barriers, and drawing inspiration from real-life stories of transformation, you are taking significant steps toward mastering the art of wealth.

Chapter 4: Income Generation Strategies

In the journey toward wealth mastery, one of the essential pillars is the ability to generate income effectively. While financial planning and a wealth mindset lay the foundation, income generation strategies fuel the engine of wealth creation. In this chapter, we will explore a wide range of income sources and strategies to boost your earning potential, emphasizing the importance of diversification and offering actionable advice for career advancement, entrepreneurship, and passive income streams.

Understanding the Dynamics of Income Generation

Income generation is not limited to a single source or method. It's a multifaceted concept encompassing various channels through which money flows into your life. Each income source has its characteristics, advantages, and challenges, making diversification a key strategy for financial success.

1. Earned Income: The Foundation of Financial Stability

Earned income is often the cornerstone of an individual's financial journey. It encompasses salaries, wages, and bonuses received from employment or self-employment. Earned income provides a sense of financial stability, allowing individuals to cover their daily expenses, save, and invest for the future.

For many, the pursuit of financial success begins with securing a job or building a career. Earned income forms the basis upon which other income sources can be built. It allows individuals to meet their immediate needs, such as housing, food, and transportation, while also contributing to their long-term financial goals.

However, there are limitations to relying solely on earned income. For one, it can be subject to fluctuations, especially in industries affected by economic downturns. Additionally, earning potential may have a ceiling, particularly if one is limited to a fixed salary or hourly wage.

To maximize the benefits of earned income, it's essential to consider strategies such as career development, skill acquisition, and salary negotiation. Advancements in one's career or business can lead to higher earnings and increased financial security. Nevertheless, for comprehensive financial success and wealth building, diversification of income sources is crucial.

2. Passive Income: The Path to Financial Freedom

Passive income is a financial lifeline that can significantly impact one's journey to wealth mastery. It represents money earned with minimal effort or direct involvement. This income source includes various streams, such as returns on investments, dividends, rental income, and royalties.

One of the key advantages of passive income is its potential to provide financial freedom and flexibility. Passive income streams can continue to flow even when you're not actively working, allowing you to enjoy more leisure time, pursue your passions, or explore new opportunities.

Building passive income typically requires initial capital and time investment. For example, investing in stocks or real estate may require upfront funds and research. However, the potential returns can far exceed the initial investment, especially when compounded over time.

Passive income can also act as a buffer against unexpected financial challenges. Having multiple passive income streams can provide a safety net, helping you maintain your financial stability during economic downturns or personal setbacks.

Diversification is essential when it comes to passive income. By spreading your investments across different asset classes, such as stocks, bonds, and real estate, you can reduce risk and increase the reliability of your passive income sources. The goal is to create a portfolio that generates consistent returns and grows over time.

3. Portfolio Income: Maximizing Investment Opportunities

Portfolio income is derived from investments in various financial instruments, including stocks, bonds, mutual funds, and exchange-traded funds (ETFs). This income source encompasses capital gains, dividends, and interest income generated by the assets within your investment portfolio.

Investing in the financial markets allows individuals to benefit from the potential growth of their investments and earn a share of corporate profits. Portfolio income is a key component of many wealth-building strategies, as it provides an opportunity to grow wealth over the long term.

Managing a diverse investment portfolio is essential for optimizing portfolio income. Diversification spreads risk across different asset classes and industries, reducing the impact of market fluctuations on your overall returns. It also allows you to capture opportunities in various sectors of the economy.

When considering portfolio income, it's important to align your investment choices with your financial goals, risk tolerance, and time horizon. For example, if you have a long-term perspective, you may opt for a more aggressive investment strategy that includes a higher allocation to stocks. Conversely, if you're seeking stability and income, a more conservative approach may include bonds and dividend-paying stocks.

Regularly reviewing and rebalancing your investment portfolio ensures that it remains aligned with your goals and risk tolerance. As your financial situation evolves, adjustments may be necessary to maintain a diversified and well-performing portfolio.

4. Business Income: Entrepreneurship as a Wealth-Building Strategy

Entrepreneurship is a dynamic and powerful means of generating income and building wealth. It involves creating and running businesses that generate profits. Business income can take various forms, including revenue from sales, service fees, and product royalties.

One of the significant advantages of entrepreneurship is the potential for substantial financial rewards. Successful entrepreneurs have the opportunity to build businesses that grow in value over time, generating significant income and wealth. Entrepreneurship also provides individuals with a sense of ownership and control over their financial destiny.

However, entrepreneurship comes with its share of challenges and risks. Starting and managing a business requires careful planning, dedication, and often financial investment. Business owners must navigate various aspects, including market research, product development, marketing, and financial management.

To succeed in entrepreneurship, individuals should consider factors such as market demand, competition, scalability, and financial sustainability. Having a clear business plan and seeking guidance from mentors or business advisors can significantly enhance the likelihood of success.

Entrepreneurship offers the potential for financial autonomy, allowing individuals to create income sources that align with their passions and interests. It can be a fulfilling and rewarding path to wealth building, provided it is approached with diligence and a commitment to continuous improvement.

5. Side Hustles and Gig Economy: Diverse Income Streams

In today's evolving workforce landscape, side hustles and participation in the gig economy have become increasingly popular ways to supplement income. Side hustles refer to additional income-generating activities pursued alongside a primary job or business, while the gig economy involves short-term, contract-based work or freelance opportunities.

Engaging in side hustles or gig economy work can be a strategic approach to diversifying income streams. It allows individuals to leverage their skills, expertise, and interests to earn extra money. Side hustles can take many forms, from freelancing as a writer or designer to offering consulting services or selling products online.

One of the benefits of side hustles and gig economy work is their flexibility. They can be pursued on a part-time basis, allowing individuals to balance multiple income sources.

Strategies for Increasing Earning Potential

To boost your earning potential, it's crucial to adopt strategies that align with your goals and circumstances. Here are actionable strategies for income generation:

1. Career Advancement: Elevating Your Income Potential

For many individuals, a significant portion of their income comes from their careers. Whether you're employed by a company or self-employed, focusing on career advancement can substantially increase your earning potential.

Career advancement involves deliberate steps to enhance your skills, expertise, and marketability in your chosen field. Here are strategies to help you climb the career ladder and boost your income:

- **Continuous Learning:** Invest in ongoing education and training. Acquiring new skills or certifications can make you a more valuable asset to your employer or clients.

- **Networking:** Build a strong professional network within your industry. Attend conferences, join industry associations, and connect with peers and mentors who can provide guidance and opportunities.

- **Performance Excellence:** Consistently deliver outstanding results in your current role. Demonstrating a strong work ethic and a commitment to excellence can lead to promotions and salary increases.

- **Negotiation Skills:** Don't underestimate the power of negotiation. When discussing compensation, be prepared to make a compelling case for why you deserve a raise or bonus. Research industry salary standards and market rates to support your argument.

- **Exploring Promotions:** If you're employed, consider seeking promotions within your organization. Advancing to higher positions often comes with increased responsibilities and, subsequently, higher compensation.

- **Side Ventures:** Explore opportunities to leverage your expertise outside of your primary job. You can offer consulting services, teach workshops, or even write a book related to your field. These side ventures can create additional income streams.

Career advancement is a long-term strategy that requires dedication and a commitment to personal growth. By continuously investing in your skills and positioning yourself as a top professional in your field, you can unlock higher earning potential and financial success.

2. Entrepreneurship: Unlocking Unlimited Income Potential

Entrepreneurship is a powerful avenue for income generation that offers virtually unlimited potential. When you start and manage your own business, you have the autonomy to control your financial destiny. Here are key considerations for aspiring entrepreneurs:

- **Passion and Expertise:** Begin by identifying your passions and areas of expertise. Your business should align with your interests and skills to maintain long-term motivation and success.

- **Market Research:** Conduct thorough market research to identify a viable business idea. Understand your target audience, competition, and market trends. A well-researched business concept is more likely to succeed.

- **Business Plan:** Develop a comprehensive business plan that outlines your business goals, strategies, and financial projections. A solid plan serves as your roadmap to success and can attract investors or lenders.

- **Financial Management:** Effective financial management is critical to business success. Budget carefully, manage expenses, and monitor cash flow to ensure your business remains financially stable.

- **Scaling:** Consider how your business can scale over time. Explore opportunities for growth, such as expanding into new markets, offering additional products or services, or franchising.

- **Risk Management:** Entrepreneurship comes with inherent risks. Evaluate risks carefully and have contingency plans in place. Seek advice from mentors or business advisors to navigate challenges.

Entrepreneurship can be a rewarding journey, allowing you to pursue your passion, create value for others, and build wealth. While it requires dedication and hard work, the potential for financial success and personal fulfillment is substantial.

3. Passive Income Investments: Growing Wealth Through Diversification

Passive income investments are an integral part of wealth building. Diversifying your investment portfolio can provide a consistent stream of income while allowing your wealth to grow over time. Here are key elements of successful passive income investments:

- **Asset Diversification:** Diversify your investment portfolio across various asset classes, such as stocks, bonds, real estate, and alternative investments. Spreading your investments reduces risk and enhances the stability of your passive income streams.

- **Regular Contributions:** Consistently contribute to your investment accounts, whether it's a retirement account, brokerage account, or a dividend reinvestment plan (DRIP). Regular contributions accelerate wealth accumulation.

- **Dividend-Paying Stocks:** Invest in dividend-paying stocks from reputable companies. These stocks not only provide potential capital appreciation but also pay regular dividends, which can significantly boost your portfolio income.

- **Bonds and Fixed-Income Investments:** Bonds offer predictable interest payments and can provide steady income. Consider bonds with varying maturities and credit qualities to diversify risk.

- **Real Estate Investment Trusts (REITs):** REITs allow you to invest in real estate without the responsibility of property management. They distribute rental income and often provide attractive yields.

- **Monitoring and Adjustment:** Regularly review your investment portfolio and make adjustments as needed. Assess your risk tolerance, investment goals, and market conditions to ensure your investments align with your objectives.

- **Tax-Efficiency:** Be mindful of tax implications when managing your investments. Strategies such as tax-efficient investing and tax-advantaged accounts can help minimize tax liabilities.

Passive income investments are a foundational element of wealth building. By taking a long-term perspective and maintaining a diversified portfolio, you can generate consistent income while preserving and growing your wealth.

4. Real Estate Investments: Rental Income and Appreciation

Investing in real estate offers the dual benefits of rental income and property appreciation. Real estate can be a valuable addition to your investment portfolio, providing both current income and potential long-term wealth growth.

Here are key considerations for real estate investments:

- **Property Selection:** Carefully choose the type of real estate investment that suits your goals. Options include residential properties, commercial properties, multifamily units, and vacation rentals.

- **Location:** Location is a critical factor in real estate. Invest in areas with strong economic fundamentals, low vacancy rates, and potential for property appreciation.

- **Property Management:** Decide whether you'll manage the property yourself or hire a property management company. Effective management is essential for maximizing rental income and property value.

- **Financing Options:** Explore financing options, such as mortgages and real estate partnerships, to acquire properties. Consider the financial implications of different financing strategies.

- **Cash Flow Analysis:** Conduct thorough cash flow analysis to determine the potential rental income and expenses associated with the property. Ensure that rental income covers operating costs and provides a positive cash flow.

- **Long-Term Strategy:** Real estate investments are typically a long-term commitment. Consider your investment horizon and how real estate fits into your overall financial plan.

- **Market Research:** Stay informed about local real estate market trends and conditions. Market dynamics can impact property values and rental income potential.

potential for property appreciation, making them a valuable asset in your wealth-building journey. Rental income from real estate investments provides a consistent cash flow, which can help cover property-related expenses, mortgage payments, and even contribute to your overall income. This reliable income source can be particularly advantageous during economic downturns when other income streams may be less predictable.

In addition to rental income, real estate investments have the potential for property appreciation over time. As demand for real estate in desirable areas increases and property values rise, the market value of your real estate holdings can grow significantly. Property appreciation adds to your overall net worth and can create opportunities for leveraging your assets in the future.

Real estate investments offer several tax advantages that can enhance their appeal. Rental income is often taxed at a lower rate than earned income, and you may be eligible for deductions related to property expenses, mortgage interest, and property depreciation. These tax benefits can further boost the financial returns on your real estate investments.

Moreover, real estate can serve as a hedge against inflation. As the cost of living increases over time, property values and rental income tend to rise as well. This means that your real estate investments can retain their purchasing power and provide a source of financial security during inflationary periods.

However, it's important to recognize that real estate investments also come with certain challenges and responsibilities. Property management can be time-consuming, and unexpected maintenance or repair costs can impact your cash flow.

Additionally, the real estate market can be cyclical, and property values may fluctuate based on economic conditions.

To mitigate these challenges and optimize the benefits of real estate investments, consider the following strategies:

- **Professional Property Management:** If managing properties yourself becomes overwhelming, consider hiring a professional property management company. They can handle tenant relations, maintenance, and other day-to-day responsibilities, allowing you to focus on your overall investment strategy.

- **Diversification:** Diversify your real estate portfolio by investing in different types of properties or geographic locations. This reduces risk and minimizes the impact of localized market downturns.

- **Long-Term Perspective:** Approach real estate investments with a long-term perspective. Property values may experience short-term fluctuations, but a well-maintained and properly managed property can appreciate significantly over time.

- **Market Research:** Stay informed about local real estate market trends and conditions. Understanding the dynamics of the areas where you invest can help you make informed decisions and identify opportunities.

- **Financing Strategies:** Explore financing options and evaluate their impact on your investment returns. Carefully consider the terms of mortgages and loans to ensure they align with your investment goals.

Real estate investments can be a valuable income source and asset class within your overall wealth-building strategy. By carefully selecting properties, managing them effectively, and maintaining a long-term perspective, you can harness the potential for rental income and property appreciation, ultimately contributing to your financial success.

5. Online Income Streams: Leveraging the Digital Age

The digital age has ushered in a multitude of online income opportunities, enabling individuals to generate income through various digital platforms and channels. These online income streams leverage skills, expertise, and creativity to reach a global audience. Here are some popular online income avenues:

- **Affiliate Marketing:** Affiliate marketing involves promoting products or services on behalf of companies and earning a commission for each sale or lead generated through your referrals. Affiliate marketers often create content, such as blog posts or videos, to attract and engage their audience.

- **E-Commerce and Dropshipping:** E-commerce allows individuals to sell products online, either through their own online store or established platforms like Amazon or Shopify. Dropshipping, a subset of e-commerce, involves selling products without holding inventory, as suppliers ship products directly to customers.

- **Online Courses and E-Learning:** If you possess expertise in a particular field or skill, consider creating and selling online courses. E-learning platforms like Udemy and Coursera provide a marketplace for course creators to reach a global audience.

- **Blogging and Content Creation:** Blogging and content creation can be monetized through advertising, sponsored content, and affiliate marketing. Successful bloggers often build a loyal readership or viewership and earn income from their content.

- **Freelance Work:** The gig economy offers numerous freelance opportunities in areas such as writing, design,

86

programming, and digital marketing. Freelancers can find work on platforms like Upwork, Fiverr, and Freelancer.

- **Digital Products and Downloads:** Create and sell digital products, such as e-books, templates, design assets, or software applications. These products can provide passive income as they can be sold repeatedly without additional effort.

- **Consulting and Coaching:** If you have specialized knowledge or skills, offer consulting or coaching services online. Many professionals provide one-on-one coaching or group coaching sessions via video conferencing platforms.

Leveraging online income streams requires a combination of skills, market research, and digital marketing strategies. Here are some tips for success in the digital realm:

- **Identify a Niche:** Find a niche or area of expertise where you can provide unique value. Specialization often leads to a more engaged and loyal audience.

- **Build an Online Presence:** Establish a strong online presence through a website, blog, social media, or YouTube channel. Consistent and valuable content helps attract and retain an audience.

- **Monetization Strategies:** Explore different monetization strategies that align with your online income stream. For example, bloggers may use a combination of advertising, sponsored content, and affiliate marketing.

online endeavors. These principles are key to building trust and credibility with your audience. Here's how to put them into practice:

- **Content Quality:** Create high-quality content that provides real value to your audience. Whether you're writing blog posts, producing videos, or offering online courses, ensure that your content is well-researched, informative, and well-presented. Quality content not only attracts and retains followers but also encourages them to share your work with others.

- **Authenticity:** Be yourself and maintain authenticity in your online presence. Share your unique perspective, experiences, and expertise. Authenticity fosters a genuine connection with your audience, as people are drawn to individuals who are relatable and sincere.

- **Transparency:** Be transparent about your affiliations, sponsorships, and any potential conflicts of interest. Transparency builds trust with your audience, and it's essential to maintain credibility in the online space.

- **Consistency:** Consistency is key to building a loyal following. Maintain a regular posting schedule or update frequency. Whether you're blogging, vlogging, or offering online services, consistency keeps your audience engaged and returning for more.

- **Engagement:** Actively engage with your audience by responding to comments, messages, and inquiries. Encourage discussions and feedback. Building a community around your online presence can lead to long-term success.

- **Adaptation:** Stay adaptable and open to change. Online platforms and trends evolve quickly. Be willing to experiment with new content formats, platforms, or strategies to keep your online income streams relevant and thriving.

Successful online income streams require dedication, patience, and the ability to adapt to an ever-changing digital landscape.

While it may take time to gain traction and see significant income, the potential for growth and financial success is substantial.

6. Multiple Income Streams: Achieving Financial Security

Diversification of income sources is a fundamental strategy for achieving financial security and wealth mastery. By building and managing multiple income streams, you can reduce financial risk, increase your overall income, and enhance your financial stability. Here's how to create a comprehensive approach to multiple income streams:

- **Primary Income Source:** Your primary income source may be earned income from your career or business. This source provides financial stability and serves as the foundation of your income strategy.

- **Secondary Income Sources:** Secondary income sources include any additional streams of income beyond your primary source. These may include side hustles, investments, or online income streams.

- **Passive Income:** Passive income sources, such as dividends from stocks or rental income from real estate, provide ongoing cash flow with minimal effort. Building a portfolio of passive income streams can significantly boost your financial security.

- **Diversification:** Diversify your income streams across different asset classes, industries, and income types. For example, a diversified investment portfolio can include stocks, bonds, and real estate. Diversification spreads risk and reduces the impact of potential setbacks.

- **Emergency Fund:** Maintain an emergency fund to cover unexpected expenses or income disruptions. Having a financial safety net ensures that you can weather financial challenges without compromising your long-term goals.

- **Regular Review:** Regularly review your income sources, financial goals, and overall financial plan. Assess the performance of each income stream and make adjustments as needed to stay on track.

- **Risk Management:** Consider risk management strategies, such as insurance or asset protection, to safeguard your income streams and assets from unexpected events.

- **Long-Term Planning:** Incorporate long-term planning into your approach to multiple income streams. Consider your retirement goals, estate planning, and wealth transfer strategies to secure your financial future.

Multiple income streams provide a robust financial foundation that can adapt to changing circumstances. Whether you're seeking to accelerate wealth accumulation, reduce financial stress, or achieve financial independence, a diversified income strategy can help you realize your objectives.

The Importance of Diversification

Diversification is a fundamental principle in income generation. It spreads risk and helps protect your financial stability. Relying solely on one income source can leave you vulnerable to economic downturns or unexpected changes in your primary source of income. By diversifying, you create a financial safety net that can weather financial storms.

Actionable Steps for Diversification

6. **Risk Assessment:** Conduct a thorough risk assessment for each income source you plan to pursue. Understand the potential risks and rewards associated with each, and evaluate how they fit into your overall financial plan.

7. **Prioritize Tax Efficiency:** Be mindful of the tax implications of your diversified income sources. Consider consulting a tax professional to optimize your tax strategy and minimize liabilities.

8. **Create a Diversification Timeline:** Develop a timeline for implementing your income diversification strategy. Determine when you will launch new income sources and how you will manage them alongside your existing ones.

9. **Allocate Resources:** Allocate resources, including time and capital, to each income source. Some may require upfront investments, while others may need consistent effort and attention.

10. **Monitoring and Evaluation:** Establish a system for monitoring and evaluating the performance of each income source. Regularly review your progress toward diversification goals and make adjustments as necessary.

11. **Network and Collaborate:** Build a network of contacts within your chosen income sources. Collaborate with others in your industry or niche to leverage opportunities and share insights.

12. **Seek Professional Advice:** Consider seeking advice from financial advisors, mentors, or industry experts who can provide guidance on income diversification strategies specific to your goals.

Embrace the Power of Diversification**

Income diversification is not just a financial strategy; it's a pathway to financial resilience and security. By spreading your income sources across various assets, industries, and opportunities, you can reduce risk, enhance your financial stability, and create a more adaptable financial portfolio.

However, diversification is not a one-time endeavor; it's an ongoing process that requires continuous assessment, learning, and adaptation. As you embark on your journey to diversify your income, keep in mind that the ultimate goal is to build a financial foundation that can withstand economic shifts, support your lifestyle, and contribute to your long-term financial success.

Remember that diversification is a reflection of your financial goals and values. It's about aligning your income sources with your aspirations and crafting a life that blends financial security with holistic well-being. By taking actionable steps toward income diversification, you are not only securing your financial future but also embracing a wealth mastery mindset that values financial choices as a means to a rich and meaningful life.

Case Studies: Diversification in Action

Let's draw inspiration from individuals who successfully diversified their income streams:

Case Study 1: The Serial Entrepreneur

Meet Mike, a dynamic individual with an entrepreneurial spirit that knows no bounds. Over the years, Mike has ventured into various business domains, ranging from tech startups to restaurant franchises. While some of his entrepreneurial endeavors faced

challenges and even outright failures, Mike's diversified approach
allowed him to not only survive but thrive in the unpredictable
world of business.

Mike's journey into entrepreneurship began with a simple idea for
a mobile app. He invested his savings, time, and energy into its
development. While the app initially struggled to gain traction,
Mike learned valuable lessons about product development,
marketing, and customer feedback. Instead of giving up, he
pivoted to a different project, a small restaurant with a unique
concept that quickly gained a loyal following.

However, the restaurant industry's unpredictability taught Mike
about the importance of risk management. He wisely decided to
invest in a third venture, a consulting firm that leveraged his
expertise in technology and entrepreneurship. This diversification
allowed him to balance the inherent risks of the restaurant
business with the stability and growth potential of consulting.

Over time, Mike continued to explore new opportunities, from e-
commerce ventures to real estate investments. His diversified
portfolio of businesses and investments provided him with
multiple income streams, making him resilient to economic
downturns and industry-specific challenges.

Today, Mike enjoys financial freedom, not because every one of
his ventures was a massive success, but because he embraced the
power of diversification. His journey teaches us that in the world
of entrepreneurship, diversifying your ventures can be a powerful
strategy for wealth accumulation and risk mitigation.

Case Study 2: The Investor's Portfolio Income

Linda, a diligent and forward-thinking investor, understood the
importance of diversification when it came to her financial goals.
She recognized that relying solely on a single income source,

such as earned income from her job, left her vulnerable to financial volatility and the whims of the job market.

To address this vulnerability, Linda embarked on a journey of financial education and investment. She diversified her investment portfolio by allocating her savings into various asset classes, including stocks, bonds, and real estate.

Linda's portfolio income strategy involved creating a well-balanced mix of assets that provided her with multiple streams of income. Here's how she approached it:

1. **Stock Investments:** Linda invested in a diversified range of stocks, including dividend-paying stocks from stable companies. This provided her with a steady stream of dividend income, which grew over time.

2. **Bonds:** Bonds formed a significant part of Linda's portfolio. Their consistent interest payments provided her with a reliable income source, and the stability of bonds helped cushion her portfolio during market downturns.

3. **Real Estate:** Linda ventured into real estate investments by purchasing rental properties. The rental income from these properties added another layer of diversification to her income sources.

4. **Retirement Accounts:** Linda maximized her contributions to retirement accounts like a 401(k) and an IRA, which not only offered tax advantages but also the potential for long-term growth.

Linda's diversified portfolio income strategy paid off in multiple ways:

- She experienced steady income even during economic downturns, thanks to the mix of assets that performed differently under various market conditions.

- Over time, her portfolio income grew, providing her with a sense of financial security and the freedom to pursue her passions and interests.

- Linda had the flexibility to adjust her investments as her financial goals evolved, whether she needed income for retirement or to fund new ventures.

Linda's story demonstrates the power of diversifying investments to create a robust and resilient income stream. By combining various asset classes, she not only protected her financial well-being but also achieved her long-term financial goals.

Case Study 3: The Online Entrepreneur

Sarah, a marketing professional with a flair for creativity, found herself drawn to the world of e-commerce. While working her full-time job, she pursued her passion for crafting handcrafted jewelry as a side project. What began as a hobby soon blossomed into a thriving online business.

Sarah's journey illustrates the potential of online entrepreneurship as a supplementary income source. Here's how she achieved her diversification goals:

1. **Passion and Expertise:** Sarah leveraged her passion for creating jewelry and her marketing expertise to establish an online store. Her unique designs and marketing savvy attracted customers from around the world.

2. **Part-Time Endeavor:** Sarah continued her full-time job while managing her e-commerce business in her free time. This

dual-income approach allowed her to maintain financial stability while growing her online venture.

3. **Gradual Growth:** Instead of rushing into full-time entrepreneurship, Sarah focused on gradual growth. She reinvested profits into her business, expanding her product line and improving customer service.

4. **Online Presence:** Sarah recognized the importance of a strong online presence. She built an engaging website, utilized social media marketing, and explored e-commerce platforms to reach a broader audience.

Over time, Sarah's online business became a significant supplementary income source. It provided her with financial flexibility, allowing her to save more, invest wisely, and pursue her long-term financial goals.

What makes Sarah's story inspiring is her ability to balance her passion with a structured approach to diversification. By keeping her full-time job while nurturing her online business, she achieved the financial stability and growth she desired. Her journey illustrates that diversifying income sources doesn't always require a complete shift in career but can be pursued as a side venture with dedication and strategic planning.

These case studies vividly illustrate the transformative power of income diversification. Each individual showcased a unique path to achieving financial stability and growth through multiple income streams. Their stories emphasize several key takeaways:

1. **Diversification Mitigates Risk:** In the world of finance, risk is ever-present. Relying solely on one income source, whether it's a job, a business, or investments, can leave you vulnerable to unexpected setbacks. Diversifying your income sources, as demonstrated by these case studies, helps mitigate

financial risks by spreading them across different assets or ventures.

2. **Balancing Passion and Practicality:** Sarah's story highlights the importance of balancing your passions with practicality. Pursuing a side hustle or passion project alongside your primary income source can be an effective way to diversify without taking unnecessary risks. It allows you to test the waters, build skills, and gradually increase your supplementary income.

3. **Strategic Investing:** Linda's success as an investor showcases the value of strategic investing. By carefully selecting a mix of assets across different categories, she created a portfolio that generated reliable income and protected her from market volatility. Her approach underscores the importance of research, asset allocation, and long-term planning.

4. **Resilience in Entrepreneurship:** Mike's entrepreneurial journey highlights the resilience required in the world of entrepreneurship. While some ventures may face challenges, maintaining a diversified portfolio of businesses allowed him to adapt, learn, and ultimately succeed. His experience emphasizes that diversifying within entrepreneurship can provide a safety net in times of uncertainty.

5. **Continuous Learning:** A common thread running through these case studies is the commitment to continuous learning. Whether it was Mike pivoting from one business to another, Linda refining her investment strategy, or Sarah honing her e-commerce skills, all three individuals dedicated themselves to acquiring new knowledge and adapting to changing circumstances.

6. **Flexibility and Adaptability:** Flexibility and adaptability are key to income diversification. Sarah's part-time venture and Mike's readiness to pivot into different industries showcase the

importance of adapting to evolving opportunities and challenges. The ability to change course when necessary is a valuable asset in achieving financial success.

7. **Financial Freedom and Choice:** Ultimately, income diversification provides individuals with financial freedom and choice. It empowers you to pursue your passions, invest in your future, and achieve your long-term financial goals without being solely dependent on one income stream.

These case studies serve as real-life examples of how income diversification can be a practical and effective strategy for achieving financial stability, growth, and resilience. Whether you're considering entrepreneurship, strategic investing, or developing supplementary income sources, their experiences offer valuable insights and inspiration on your own journey to financial success.

Navigating the Landscape of Income Generation

Income generation is a dynamic and multifaceted aspect of the wealth-building journey. To achieve financial success and mastery, it's crucial to explore diverse income sources and strategies that align with your goals. Whether you focus on career advancement, entrepreneurship, passive income, or a combination of these strategies, remember the importance of diversification. Diversifying your income sources not only enhances your financial stability but also opens doors to new opportunities for wealth creation.

In the chapters that follow, we will delve deeper into specific income generation strategies, providing insights and actionable steps to help you maximize your earning potential and move closer to your financial aspirations.

Chapter 5: Smart Saving and Investing

As we continue our journey to wealth mastery, we arrive at a pivotal crossroad—smart saving and investing. These two pillars are the engines that power long-term wealth accumulation. In this chapter, we will delve into the principles of saving and investing wisely, explore various investment vehicles such as stocks, real estate, and retirement accounts, and discuss the critical aspects of risk management on the path to building substantial wealth.

The Art of Saving: A Foundation for Wealth

Saving is the bedrock upon which financial security and wealth accumulation are built. It's a discipline that allows you to set aside a portion of your income for future use, emergencies, and investment opportunities. Let's explore the principles of smart saving:

Savings are the cornerstone of financial security and wealth building. They provide the foundation upon which you can build a stable and prosperous future. The principles and strategies outlined in this chapter are essential for nurturing your savings and realizing your financial goals. Let's delve deeper into each of these principles:

1. Pay Yourself First: A Non-Negotiable Priority

The concept of "paying yourself first" is a powerful and transformative savings principle. It revolves around the idea that before you allocate money to cover expenses, bills, or discretionary spending, you should allocate a portion of your income to savings. In essence, you treat your savings as a non-negotiable expense, just like rent or utilities. By making saving a priority, you ensure that you're consistently setting money aside for your future.

This principle aligns with the notion that your financial future should take precedence over immediate desires or lifestyle upgrades. It encourages discipline and self-control in managing your finances. When you commit to paying yourself first, you're laying the groundwork for financial security, enabling you to build emergency funds, invest for retirement, and work toward other important financial goals.

2. Crafting Your Financial Roadmap: The Importance of Budgeting

A budget is your financial roadmap, guiding you toward your financial destination. It serves as a comprehensive plan that outlines your income and expenses, offering a clear picture of your financial health. Here's why budgeting is a crucial component of your savings strategy:

A. Income Tracking: A budget helps you track your sources of income, whether they come from your job, investments, side hustles, or other avenues. Knowing your exact income allows you to allocate funds more effectively.

B. Expense Management: A budget categorizes and tracks your expenses, shedding light on where your money is going. It helps you identify areas where you can cut costs or redirect funds toward savings.

C. Setting Priorities: With a budget, you can establish financial priorities. It enables you to allocate specific amounts of your income to savings, debt repayment, living expenses, and discretionary spending.

D. Goal Setting: Your budget is where you define clear savings goals. Whether you're saving for an emergency fund, a home down payment, or your child's education, your budget ensures that you allocate funds toward these objectives.

E. Monitoring and Adjustment: A budget isn't a one-time exercise; it's an ongoing tool. Regularly reviewing and adjusting your budget is essential to staying on track and accommodating changing financial circumstances.

By crafting a budget and consistently following it, you gain control over your financial life. It's a proactive approach to financial management that empowers you to make informed decisions and achieve your financial objectives.

3. The Power of Clear Savings Goals

Setting clear and specific savings goals is like setting coordinates on your financial map. These goals provide motivation, direction, and a sense of purpose to your savings efforts. Without well-defined goals, saving money may lack purpose, making it easier to stray from your financial path.

Consider the following types of savings goals:

A. Emergency Fund: One of your primary savings goals should be establishing an emergency fund. This fund serves as a financial safety net, covering unexpected expenses such as medical bills, car repairs, or unexpected job loss. A common recommendation is to aim for three to six months' worth of living expenses in your emergency fund.

B. Short-Term Goals: Short-term savings goals typically have a time frame of one to two years. Examples include saving for a vacation, purchasing a new computer, or funding home repairs.

101

C. Medium-Term Goals: Medium-term goals span one to five years and often involve more significant expenses, such as saving for a down payment on a home or funding your child's education.

D. Long-Term Goals: Long-term savings goals extend beyond five years and may encompass major life events like retirement planning, creating generational wealth, or achieving financial independence.

By establishing clear savings goals within these categories, you provide yourself with both short-term gratification and long-term financial security. These goals act as milestones along your financial journey, giving you a sense of accomplishment as you achieve them.

4. The Beauty of Automation: Effortless Saving

Saving money doesn't have to be a laborious or burdensome task. Automation is a powerful tool that can make saving virtually effortless. By setting up automatic transfers from your checking account to your savings account, you ensure that a portion of your income is consistently saved without requiring your active participation.

Automation offers several advantages:

A. Consistency: Automated transfers occur on a predefined schedule, ensuring that you save consistently. This consistency is essential for building a substantial nest egg over time.

B. Simplicity: Once you've set up automated transfers, there's no need to manually initiate savings. It simplifies the process, reducing the temptation to skip or delay savings contributions.

C. Psychological Benefits: Automation removes the temptation to spend money that's readily available in your checking account. It's a safeguard against impulsive purchases that can derail your savings efforts.

D. Time Savings: Automation frees up your time and mental energy. Instead of repeatedly deciding how much to save and when, you set it up once and let the process run in the background.

E. Peace of Mind: Knowing that you're consistently saving provides peace of mind. It helps you feel secure in your financial future, even during times of economic uncertainty.

Whether you're saving for short-term goals like a vacation or long-term goals like retirement, automation ensures that you're making steady progress toward your objectives. It's a tool that makes financial success more achievable and convenient.

5. Debt Reduction: A Savings Catalyst

While it might seem counterintuitive, paying off debt is a potent strategy for enhancing your savings. High-interest debt, such as credit card balances or personal loans, can drain your financial resources through interest payments. By prioritizing debt reduction, you can achieve two critical financial objectives:

A. Interest Savings: Eliminating high-interest debt frees up more of your income. The money that would have gone toward interest payments can now be redirected to savings and investments.

B. Debt-Free Lifestyle: Reducing or eliminating debt positions you for a more financially secure future. Without the burden of debt, you have more financial freedom and flexibility.

This newfound freedom allows you to allocate a larger portion of your income to savings, investments, and achieving your financial goals.

C. Improve Credit Score: Reducing debt can improve your credit score over time. A higher credit score not only opens doors to better financial opportunities but can also lead to lower interest rates on future loans, reducing the overall cost of borrowing.

D. Peace of Mind: Living a debt-free lifestyle provides peace of mind. You won't constantly worry about debt payments, collection calls, or late fees. This financial peace allows you to focus on growing your savings and pursuing your financial aspirations.

Remember that debt reduction is not limited to high-interest debt. It's a sound financial strategy even for lower-interest debt like mortgages or student loans. Reducing and eventually eliminating these obligations can significantly contribute to your long-term financial well-being.

The principles and strategies outlined in this chapter are essential for nurturing your savings and realizing your financial goals. By prioritizing paying yourself first, creating a budget, setting clear savings goals, automating savings, and reducing debt, you lay the foundation for a secure financial future. These practices empower you to take control of your finances, make informed decisions, and work toward achieving your financial aspirations.

Savings are the building blocks of wealth, and they play a pivotal role in creating a prosperous and financially secure life. The journey to financial success begins with these fundamental principles, setting the stage for more advanced wealth-building strategies explored in later chapters. In the following chapters, we will delve deeper into the strategies for effective investing, risk management, and long-term wealth accumulation. Together, these elements will form a comprehensive framework for mastering wealth and achieving your financial dreams.

Investing for Wealth Accumulation

While saving provides the foundation, investing is the vehicle that accelerates wealth accumulation. It involves putting your money to work by acquiring assets that have the potential to appreciate in value or generate income. Here are insights into different investment vehicles:

7. Commodities: Commodities are physical goods like gold, oil, or agricultural products. Investing in commodities can provide diversification and a hedge against inflation.

8. Collectibles: Collectibles, such as art, antiques, or rare coins, can be alternative investments. Their value can appreciate over time, but they lack liquidity and may require expertise for valuation.

9. Peer-to-Peer Lending: This form of investment involves lending money to individuals or businesses through online platforms. It offers potential returns in the form of interest payments.

10. Cryptocurrencies: Cryptocurrencies like Bitcoin have gained popularity as alternative investments. They are highly volatile and speculative, making them a high-risk option.

Each of these investment options comes with its unique characteristics, advantages, and risks. The key to effective investment is diversification. By spreading your investments across different asset classes, you can reduce risk and enhance the potential for consistent returns over time.

1. Stocks: Investing in stocks represents one of the most common ways to participate in the financial markets. When you buy a stock, you acquire ownership in a company, and your returns are tied to the company's performance. Stocks can offer the potential for capital appreciation as well as dividends, which are typically paid out of a company's profits.

Diversifying your stock portfolio is essential to manage risk effectively. While individual stocks can be volatile, spreading your investments across different industries, sectors, and geographic regions can help mitigate the impact of poor performance in any one area. This diversification can provide a more stable and balanced portfolio, allowing you to weather market fluctuations more comfortably.

2. Real Estate: Real estate has long been a favored investment choice. It involves purchasing physical properties such as residential or commercial real estate with the expectation of generating rental income and/or capital appreciation. Real estate can be an excellent way to diversify your investment portfolio and provide a potential hedge against inflation.

Additionally, real estate investments often offer tax benefits. Mortgage interest and property taxes are typically deductible expenses, and real estate investors may also take advantage of depreciation deductions. However, real estate investments require careful research, management, and capital for property acquisition and maintenance.

3. Retirement Accounts: Retirement accounts like 401(k)s and IRAs are specifically designed to encourage long-term retirement savings. One of the primary advantages of these accounts is the potential for tax benefits. Contributions to traditional 401(k)s and IRAs are often tax-deductible, reducing your taxable income in the year of the contribution.

Moreover, the earnings within these accounts grow tax-deferred until withdrawal, allowing your investments to potentially compound more effectively. Many employers offer 401(k) plans with matching contributions, which is essentially free money. It's wise to take full advantage of these matching contributions to maximize your retirement savings.

4. Bonds: Bonds are debt securities issued by governments, municipalities, or corporations. When you invest in bonds, you are essentially lending money to the issuer in exchange for periodic interest payments and the return of the principal amount at maturity. Bonds are typically considered lower risk compared to stocks and can provide a level of income stability to a diversified portfolio.

Bonds come in various forms, including government bonds, municipal bonds, corporate bonds, and Treasury bonds. The risk associated with bonds varies depending on the issuer's creditworthiness. Government bonds are often considered low-risk, while corporate bonds may carry higher credit risk. Bonds can play a crucial role in balancing the risk in a diversified investment portfolio.

5. Mutual Funds and ETFs: Mutual funds and exchange-traded funds (ETFs) are investment vehicles that pool money from multiple investors to purchase a diversified portfolio of stocks, bonds, or other assets. These investment options offer several advantages, including diversification, professional management, and liquidity.

Mutual funds are actively managed by professional fund managers who make investment decisions on behalf of the fund's investors. ETFs, on the other hand, typically passively track an index or a specific asset class. Both options provide investors with easy access to a diversified portfolio without the need for individual stock or bond selection.

6. Entrepreneurship: Entrepreneurship involves starting, owning, or investing in businesses with the expectation of generating profits. This form of investment can offer substantial rewards, including unlimited income potential, creative control, and the opportunity to build valuable assets.

However, entrepreneurship also comes with significant risks. New businesses often face challenges, including competition, market fluctuations, and operational issues. It requires careful planning, market research, and a willingness to adapt to changing circumstances. Successful entrepreneurship can lead to financial independence and wealth accumulation, but it's essential to approach it with a clear strategy and a well-thought-out business plan.

7. Commodities: Commodities are physical goods that can be bought and sold, such as gold, oil, grains, and metals. Investing in commodities can provide diversification benefits, as their performance may not always correlate with traditional financial markets like stocks and bonds.

Commodities can serve as a hedge against inflation, as their prices may rise in response to economic factors. For example, gold is often considered a store of value during times of economic uncertainty. However, commodities can also be volatile and may require specialized knowledge or investment vehicles like commodity futures contracts.

8. Collectibles: Collectibles, such as art, antiques, rare coins, or vintage cars, represent alternative investments that can appreciate in value over time. These assets can add diversity to your investment portfolio and may appeal to individuals with a passion for collecting.

Investing in collectibles, however, comes with unique challenges. Valuing collectible assets can be subjective, and their liquidity may be limited. Additionally, the market for collectibles can be niche and influenced by trends and tastes, making it important to conduct thorough research before investing.

9. Peer-to-Peer Lending: Peer-to-peer (P2P) Lending is a modern investment avenue that leverages online platforms to connect borrowers with individual investors. In P2P lending, you act as a lender, providing funds to borrowers seeking personal loans, small business loans, or other types of financing. These platforms often have their credit rating systems and risk assessment processes.

One of the advantages of P2P lending is the potential for attractive returns compared to traditional savings accounts or bonds. Depending on the platform and the risk level you choose, you can earn competitive interest rates on your investments. P2P lending also allows you to diversify your investments across various loans, reducing the impact of defaults on your overall returns.

However, it's essential to understand that P2P lending involves risk. Borrowers may default on their loans, leading to potential losses for lenders. Therefore, diversifying your P2P lending investments across multiple loans and risk levels is crucial to mitigate this risk. Additionally, it's essential to carefully review the terms and conditions of P2P lending platforms and conduct thorough due diligence on borrowers.

10. Cryptocurrencies: Cryptocurrencies represent a relatively new and highly speculative investment class. These digital or virtual currencies use cryptography for security and operate independently of traditional financial institutions. Bitcoin, Ethereum, and other cryptocurrencies have gained popularity among investors.

The appeal of cryptocurrencies lies in their potential for high returns, especially during periods of rapid price appreciation. However, they are also known for their extreme price volatility. Investing in cryptocurrencies carries a substantial risk of price fluctuations, and it's possible to experience significant gains or losses in a short period.

If you choose to invest in cryptocurrencies, it's essential to approach them with caution and diligence. Understand the technology and underlying principles of cryptocurrencies, and consider them as a speculative asset within your overall investment portfolio. Cryptocurrencies should be part of a well-diversified strategy, and you should only invest what you can afford to lose.

The investment landscape offers a wide array of opportunities to build and grow wealth. The key to successful investing is diversification, risk management, and a clear understanding of your financial goals and risk tolerance. Depending on your preferences and circumstances, you can choose from various asset classes, from traditional investments like stocks and bonds to alternative options like real estate, entrepreneurship, or cryptocurrencies.

Your investment strategy should align with your financial goals, investment timeline, and risk appetite. Consider seeking guidance from financial professionals or advisors to help you develop a well-rounded and diversified investment portfolio. Remember that investing is a long-term endeavor, and patience, discipline, and ongoing learning are essential for achieving your financial objectives while managing risk effectively.

Risk Management and Wealth Accumulation

Investing carries inherent risks, and managing these risks is paramount to long-term wealth accumulation. Here are key risk management strategies:

Investing is a journey, not a destination, and it's essential to approach it with a well-thought-out strategy that aligns with your financial goals, risk tolerance, and timeline. Whether you're a novice investor or have years of experience, adhering to fundamental principles can help you make informed and prudent investment decisions.

1. Diversification: The Foundation of Sound Investing

Diversification is a core principle of investment strategy, and for a good reason. It's like not putting all your eggs in one basket. By spreading your investments across different asset classes and sectors, you reduce the risk associated with any single investment. This means that if one asset class or sector experiences a downturn, the impact on your overall portfolio is minimized.

Diversification can take various forms:

- **Asset Class Diversification:** Allocate your investments across various asset classes, such as stocks, bonds, real estate, and cash equivalents. Each asset class has its risk-return profile, and combining them can help balance your portfolio.

- **Sector Diversification:** Within asset classes like stocks, diversify across sectors like technology, healthcare, finance, and consumer goods. This minimizes your exposure to sector-specific risks.

- **Geographic Diversification:** Consider international investments to reduce the impact of country-specific economic conditions and geopolitical events.

- **Investment Vehicle Diversification:** Utilize different investment vehicles like mutual funds, exchange-traded funds (ETFs), and individual securities to access various assets.

Diversification doesn't guarantee profits or protect against losses, but it does help manage risk. It's the investment equivalent of not putting all your eggs in one basket.

2. Know Your Risk Tolerance

Understanding your risk tolerance is crucial when building an investment portfolio. Risk tolerance refers to your ability and willingness to endure the ups and downs of the market without panicking or making impulsive decisions.

Your risk tolerance depends on several factors:

- **Age:** Generally, younger investors can afford to take more risk because they have a longer investment horizon to recover from market downturns. Older investors nearing retirement may prefer a more conservative approach to preserve capital.

- **Financial Goals:** Your financial objectives play a significant role in determining your risk tolerance. If your goal is long-term wealth accumulation, you may be comfortable with a higher level of risk. In contrast, if you're saving for a short-term goal or need capital preservation, lower-risk investments may be more appropriate.

- **Comfort with Volatility:** Consider your emotional response to market volatility. If you lose sleep over market fluctuations, it may be an indicator that your risk tolerance is lower.

Assessing your risk tolerance can involve self-reflection and sometimes consultation with a financial advisor. It's essential to choose investments that align with your comfort level, as this can help you stay committed to your long-term investment strategy.

3. Conduct Thorough Research and Due Diligence

Investing requires diligence and research. Before committing your hard-earned money to any investment, take the time to understand what you're investing in and the associated risks. Due diligence is essential for making informed investment decisions.

Here are some steps to conduct thorough research and due diligence:

- **Asset Analysis:** Understand the fundamentals of the asset you're considering. For stocks, this may include analyzing financial statements, evaluating the company's competitive position, and studying industry trends. For real estate, assess property values, location, and potential rental income.

- **Risk Assessment:** Identify and assess the risks associated with the investment. Consider factors like market risk, credit risk (for bonds), liquidity risk, and geopolitical risk (for international investments).

- **Historical Performance:** Review the historical performance of the asset or investment vehicle. Past performance is not indicative of future results, but it can provide insights into how the investment has fared in different market conditions.

- **Fees and Costs:** Understand the fees and costs associated with the investment. High fees can erode your returns over time, so it's essential to factor them into your decision.

- **Investment Horizon:** Consider your investment horizon. Some investments are better suited for long-term goals, while others may be more appropriate for short-term objectives.

- **Regulatory Compliance:** Ensure that the investment and the investment provider comply with relevant regulations and laws.

- **Alternative Investments:** Be cautious when considering alternative investments, such as hedge funds, private equity, or cryptocurrencies. These often come with higher complexity and risk, and thorough due diligence is essential.

- **Professional Advice:** In complex investment situations, or if you're uncertain about your ability to conduct due diligence effectively, consider seeking advice from financial professionals or advisors. They can provide valuable insights and guidance.

4. Embrace a Long-Term Perspective

Investing is not a get-rich-quick scheme; it's a long-term journey. Market fluctuations, economic cycles, and geopolitical events are part of the investment landscape. To navigate these ups and downs successfully, it's crucial to adopt a long-term perspective.

Historically, the stock market and other asset classes have shown an upward trajectory over the long term, despite periodic downturns. By focusing on your long-term goals and maintaining discipline during market turbulence, you're more likely to benefit from the potential growth opportunities that investments offer.

Here are some key aspects of embracing a long-term perspective:

- **Market Volatility is Normal:** Stock markets are inherently volatile, with prices fluctuating daily due to various factors. While these fluctuations can be unnerving, they are a natural part of investing. Instead of reacting to short-term market movements, stay focused on your long-term goals.

- **Time in the Market Matters:** The longer your money remains invested, the more it benefits from the power of compounding. Compounding allows your investment gains to generate additional gains over time. This exponential growth effect is more pronounced in long-term investments.

- **Diversification Helps Ride Out Volatility:** Diversification becomes even more critical when you have a long-term perspective. It helps cushion your portfolio against the impact of severe market swings. Over time, a diversified portfolio is more likely to deliver stable returns and reduce the risk of substantial losses.

- **Market Timing is Challenging:** Attempting to time the market—buying when you think prices are low and selling when you believe they are high—is a challenging and often futile endeavor. Even seasoned professionals struggle with market timing. Instead, focus on your asset allocation and stay invested through market cycles.

- **Regular Contributions:** A long-term perspective aligns well with a strategy of making regular contributions to your investments. Dollar-cost averaging involves investing a fixed amount at regular intervals, regardless of market conditions. This approach can reduce the impact of market volatility on your overall investment performance.

- **Periodic Portfolio Review:** While you should maintain a long-term perspective, it's essential to periodically review your portfolio to ensure it aligns with your goals and risk tolerance. Over time, your financial situation and objectives may change, necessitating adjustments to your investments.

- **Stay Informed:** Staying informed about broader economic trends, global events, and market developments can help you make informed decisions. However, avoid the temptation to react impulsively to short-term news.

5. Maintain an Emergency Fund

Even the best investment strategy can be derailed by unexpected financial emergencies or setbacks. To safeguard your investments and avoid premature liquidation during challenging times, maintain an emergency fund.

An emergency fund is a dedicated savings account that covers essential living expenses for a specific period, typically three to six months. It acts as a financial cushion during unexpected events, such as medical emergencies, job loss, or major home repairs. By having an emergency fund, you reduce the need to dip into your investments when you encounter unforeseen expenses.

Here are some key considerations for your emergency fund:

- **Savings Target:** Aim to save at least three to six months' worth of living expenses in your emergency fund. The exact amount depends on your circumstances and risk tolerance. If you have dependents or work in an industry with uncertain job prospects, consider a more substantial fund.

- **Liquid and Accessible:** Ensure that your emergency fund is readily accessible, typically in a high-yield savings account or money market fund. The goal is to have quick access to funds when needed.

- **Separate from Investments:** Keep your emergency fund separate from your investment accounts. Mixing the two can lead to impulsive decisions during market downturns.

- **Regular Review:** Periodically review and replenish your emergency fund as needed. Life circumstances, such as changes in income or expenses, may necessitate adjustments.

Having an emergency fund not only provides financial security but also supports your long-term investment strategy by allowing your investments to remain untouched during challenging times.

6. Consider Professional Advice

Investing can become increasingly complex as your financial situation evolves or when you have specific financial goals, such as retirement planning, estate planning, or tax optimization. In such cases, seeking professional advice can be a valuable resource.

Here are situations where professional advice may be beneficial:

- **Retirement Planning:** Preparing for retirement involves various considerations, including investment allocation, withdrawal strategies, and Social Security optimization. A financial advisor can help you create a retirement plan tailored to your needs.

- **Tax Planning:** Tax-efficient investing is essential for maximizing returns. Tax professionals can advise you on strategies to minimize your tax liability while adhering to tax laws.

- **Estate Planning:** Estate planning involves decisions about passing on your assets to heirs, minimizing estate taxes, and establishing trusts or wills. Estate planning attorneys can provide guidance in this complex area.

- **Complex Investments:** If you're considering alternative investments, complex financial products, or sophisticated strategies, professional advice is often necessary. These investments may involve higher risks and require specialized knowledge.

- **Life Changes:** Significant life events, such as marriage, divorce, the birth of children, or the death of a loved one, can have profound financial implications. Seeking advice during these transitions can help you navigate financial changes effectively.

When selecting a financial advisor or professional, ensure they have appropriate credentials, experience, and a fiduciary responsibility to act in your best interests. Additionally, establish clear communication and transparency about your financial goals and risk tolerance.

Case Studies in Wealth Accumulation

Let's draw inspiration from individuals who used smart saving and investing strategies to accumulate wealth:

Case Study 1: The Consistent Investor - Mark's Path to Financial Success

Mark's journey to financial success began with a commitment to consistency. Early in his career, he recognized the importance of investing as a means of securing his financial future. Here, we delve into Mark's approach to investing, the challenges he faced, and the rewards he reaped over time.

Starting Early and Regular Contributions

Mark understood that time is a crucial factor in building wealth through investments. In his 20s, he started investing in the stock market, allocating a portion of his monthly income toward his investment portfolio. This early start gave him a significant advantage because it allowed his investments more time to grow.

118

Diversification and Risk Management

Mark recognized the importance of diversification in his investment strategy. Rather than putting all his eggs in one basket, he spread his investments across various asset classes, including stocks, bonds, and real estate investment trusts (REITs). This diversification helped mitigate risk and reduce the impact of market fluctuations on his portfolio.

Staying Invested Through Market Fluctuations

One of the most challenging aspects of investing is the emotional rollercoaster that comes with market volatility. Mark, however, had the discipline to stay invested through market ups and downs. He understood that trying to time the market or reacting impulsively to short-term fluctuations could lead to missed opportunities and reduced returns.

Continuous Learning and Adaptation

Mark's journey as an investor was marked by a commitment to continuous learning. He regularly read books, attended seminars, and stayed informed about market trends and economic developments. This knowledge empowered him to make informed investment decisions and adapt his strategy as needed.

Achieving Financial Goals and Retirement

Over the years, Mark's disciplined approach to investing paid off. His investment portfolio grew steadily, and he reached many of his financial goals. When he decided to retire, he had the financial security and peace of mind to do so comfortably.

Mark's story demonstrates the power of consistency, diversification, and discipline in building wealth over time. His early start and commitment to his financial future allowed him to achieve his retirement dreams and enjoy the fruits of his long-term investment strategy.

Case Study 2: The Real Estate Investor - Lisa's Path to Wealth Through Property

Lisa's journey to financial success took a unique path through real estate investing. Her story showcases how a carefully chosen and managed real estate portfolio can contribute significantly to one's net worth and financial security.

Beginning the Real Estate Journey

In her 30s, Lisa decided to invest in real estate by purchasing her first rental property. She saw real estate as an opportunity to diversify her investments and generate rental income while benefiting from potential property appreciation.

Property Selection and Location

One of Lisa's key strategies was meticulous property selection. She conducted thorough research on the housing market, focusing on areas with high demand for rentals. Her properties were strategically located near schools, public transportation, and amenities, making them attractive to tenants.

Diligent Property Management

Managing rental properties can be demanding, but Lisa was committed to maintaining her investments. She ensured her properties were well-maintained, responsive to tenant needs, and in compliance with local regulations. Her dedication to providing quality housing contributed to tenant satisfaction and tenant retention.

Rental Income and Property Appreciation

Lisa's real estate portfolio began to generate rental income, providing her with a steady stream of earnings. Additionally, over the years, her properties appreciated in value due to factors such as location, renovations, and market conditions. This dual benefit of rental income and property appreciation significantly contributed to her net worth.

Continued Investment and Expansion

As Lisa's real estate investments proved successful, she continued to expand her portfolio. She reinvested her rental income into acquiring additional properties. Her approach was strategic, focusing on properties with the potential for both rental income and long-term appreciation.

Achieving Financial Security and Freedom

Lisa's dedication to real estate investing paid off over time. Her rental income grew, and her properties appreciated, steadily increasing her net worth. By the time she reached her financial goals, she had achieved a level of financial security that allowed her to enjoy her desired lifestyle and retire comfortably.

Lisa's story highlights the potential of real estate as an investment vehicle when chosen and managed thoughtfully. Her commitment to property selection, diligent management, and continued investment allowed her to leverage the benefits of real estate to achieve her financial dreams.

Case Study 3: The Retirement Savvy Professional - John's Path to Financial Security

John's journey to financial security revolved around diligent retirement planning and making the most of employer-sponsored retirement accounts. His story illustrates how maximizing retirement contributions, diversifying investments, and taking advantage of employer benefits can pave the way for a secure retirement.

Maximizing Retirement Contributions

Early in his career, John recognized the importance of saving for retirement. He took full advantage of his employer's retirement plan, contributing a significant portion of his salary. His consistent contributions allowed him to benefit from the power of compounding over time.

**Diversification and Asset Allocation

**

John was diligent about diversifying his retirement account investments. He spread his contributions across various asset classes, including stocks, bonds, and mutual funds. This diversification helped reduce the risk associated with any single investment and provided balance to his retirement portfolio.

Employer Matching Contributions

One of the key features of John's employer-sponsored retirement plan was the employer match. His employer matched a portion of his contributions, effectively doubling his retirement savings. John recognized the importance of this benefit and ensured he contributed enough to maximize the employer match.

Regular Account Review and Adjustments

While John maintained a long-term perspective in his retirement planning, he also periodically reviewed and adjusted his retirement account. He rebalanced his investments to align with his changing risk tolerance and financial goals. This proactive approach allowed him to optimize his retirement savings.

Retirement Security and Peace of Mind

As John approached retirement age, he had accumulated a substantial retirement nest egg. His disciplined approach to retirement planning, combined with employer matching contributions and diversified investments, provided him with financial security and peace of mind in retirement.

John's story underscores the significance of maximizing retirement contributions, diversifying investments, and taking advantage of employer benefits in achieving financial security during retirement. His commitment to long-term planning allowed him to enjoy a retirement free from financial worries.

These case studies demonstrate that there is no one-size-fits-all approach to achieving financial success. Whether through consistent investing in various asset classes, strategic real estate acquisitions, or diligent retirement planning, individuals can realize their financial aspirations with careful planning, discipline, and a long-term perspective. Each path to success is unique, emphasizing the importance of aligning one's investment strategy with personal goals and circumstances.

Navigating the Path to Wealth Accumulation

Smart saving and investing are the engines of wealth accumulation, enabling you to grow your wealth over time. By adopting the principles of saving, exploring various investment vehicles, and managing risk effectively, you can chart a course toward financial security and long-term prosperity.

Chapter 6: Debt Management and Financial Freedom

In our quest for wealth mastery, one critical aspect that often demands our attention is debt management. Debt can either be a powerful tool for wealth creation or a heavy burden that hinders financial progress. In this chapter, we will address the role of debt in wealth building and how to manage it effectively. We'll also share strategies for debt reduction and achieving financial independence, as well as offer guidance on living below your means and building a savings cushion.

Debt as a Double-Edged Sword

Debt is a financial instrument that allows individuals to access resources they may not have immediately. It can be used to invest in education, buy a home, start a business, or cover emergencies. However, the way debt is managed determines whether it's a catalyst for wealth or an obstacle to financial freedom.

Good Debt vs. Bad Debt: Navigating the Path to Wealth

Debt is a double-edged sword in the world of personal finance. When used wisely, it can serve as a powerful tool for wealth creation and financial growth. However, if mismanaged, debt can become a heavy burden that impedes progress toward financial goals. To harness the potential of debt effectively, one must understand the distinction between good debt and bad debt and learn how to leverage them strategically.

1. Good Debt: A Stepping Stone to Wealth

Good debt, as the name implies, is a type of debt that can contribute positively to your financial well-being and wealth-building endeavors. It is characterized by the acquisition of assets that have the potential to appreciate in value or generate income over time. Let's explore some common forms of good debt and how they can play a pivotal role in wealth creation.

a. Mortgage Debt: The Pathway to Homeownership

For many individuals and families, purchasing a home is a significant financial goal. Mortgage debt is a prime example of good debt, as it allows people to acquire an appreciating asset: real estate. Homeownership not only provides shelter but also builds equity as property values tend to appreciate over the long term. Additionally, mortgage interest payments may offer tax benefits, further enhancing the financial advantages of homeownership.

b. Student Loans: Investing in Education

Education is often regarded as one of the most valuable investments a person can make. Student loans, when used to finance higher education, are a form of good debt. They enable individuals to acquire knowledge, skills, and credentials that can lead to higher earning potential and career opportunities. Over time, the return on investment from education can far exceed the cost of student loans.

c. Business Loans: Fueling Entrepreneurship

Entrepreneurs and small business owners often rely on loans to fund the establishment or expansion of their enterprises. These business loans can be considered good debt because they are used to invest in income-generating assets – the businesses themselves. When managed effectively, a well-run business can not only repay its loans but also generate profits and contribute to the owner's wealth.

2. Bad Debt: The Pitfalls of Consumer Borrowing

On the other side of the debt spectrum lies bad debt, which is incurred for expenses that do not contribute to wealth creation or generate income. Bad debt often results from impulsive or frivolous spending, and it can become a financial trap that hinders individuals from achieving their financial goals.

a. High-Interest Credit Card Debt: A Costly Culprit

One of the most notorious forms of bad debt is high-interest credit card debt. When individuals use credit cards to finance non-essential purchases, especially if they carry a balance from month to month, they subject themselves to exorbitant interest rates. The interest payments on such debt can quickly accumulate and become a significant financial burden.

b. Consumer Loans for Depreciating Assets

Taking out loans for consumer goods that rapidly lose value, such as luxury cars, electronics, or vacations, falls under the category of bad debt. These loans do not contribute to wealth creation and may result in individuals paying more for an item in interest than its actual worth over time.

c. Excessive Personal Loans: Borrowing for Lifestyle

Personal loans taken out for lifestyle enhancements, such as extravagant vacations, designer clothing, or extravagant home renovations, often lead to bad debt. These loans do not generate income or appreciating assets and can lead to a cycle of overborrowing and financial stress.

Leveraging Debt Strategically: Key Considerations

Understanding the distinction between good debt and bad debt is a crucial first step toward making informed financial decisions. However, it's essential to recognize that the utilization of debt is

126

not inherently good or bad. Instead, it depends on how effectively and strategically debt is managed and employed. Here are some key considerations when leveraging debt as a wealth-building tool:

1. Interest Rates and Terms:

One of the most critical factors when evaluating debt is the interest rate associated with it. Lower-interest loans, such as mortgages and some student loans, can be more manageable and may offer tax benefits. Conversely, high-interest debt, like credit card balances, can quickly spiral out of control due to compounding interest.

2. Investment Potential:

Consider the potential return on investment (ROI) of the assets acquired with debt. Good debt should be used to finance assets that have the potential to appreciate or generate income that exceeds the cost of borrowing. Evaluating the ROI can help determine whether the debt is worth taking on.

3. Cash Flow Management:

Before taking on any debt, it's crucial to assess your cash flow and budget. Ensure that you have a clear plan for making debt payments without sacrificing your ability to cover essential living expenses, savings, and investments.

4. Risk Tolerance:

Assess your risk tolerance when using debt for investments. While investments like stocks and real estate have the potential for significant returns, they also come with risks, including market volatility. Make sure you are comfortable with the level of risk associated with your investments.

5. Emergency Fund:

Maintaining an emergency fund is essential when managing debt. It serves as a financial safety net, ensuring that you have funds available to cover unexpected expenses or debt payments in times of financial hardship.

6. Debt Reduction Strategies:

If you carry high-interest debt, such as credit card balances, develop a plan to pay it off as soon as possible. Debt reduction strategies, such as the debt snowball or debt avalanche methods, can help you eliminate bad debt systematically.

7. Professional Advice:

Consider seeking guidance from financial advisors or professionals, especially when dealing with complex debt management or investment decisions. Their expertise can provide valuable insights and help you navigate the complexities of financial planning.

Case Study 1: Leveraging Mortgage Debt for Wealth

John and Mary, a young couple, decided to purchase their first home. They carefully assessed their finances and took out a mortgage to buy a house in a desirable neighborhood. While the mortgage was a significant financial commitment, they saw it as a form of good debt. Over the years, the value of their home appreciated steadily, and they enjoyed the benefits of homeownership.

As they paid down their mortgage, their equity in the home increased. They eventually refinanced their mortgage to a lower interest rate, reducing their monthly payments and freeing up more cash flow. They used the additional funds to invest in a diversified portfolio of stocks and bonds.

By leveraging mortgage debt strategically, John and Mary not only acquired a valuable asset in the form of their home but also created an investment portfolio that generated passive income. This combination of good debt and wise investing helped them build wealth over time.

Case Study 2: The Pitfalls of High-Interest Credit Card Debt

Emily, a recent college graduate, found herself in a challenging financial situation due to credit card debt. During her college years, she had accumulated high-interest credit card balances while financing her lifestyle expenses. The interest rates on these balances were exorbitant, and the monthly minimum payments barely made a dent in the principal.

Recognizing the need for a financial turnaround, Emily embarked on a debt reduction journey. She created a strict budget, focusing on essentials and eliminating discretionary spending. Emily also explored balance transfer offers with lower interest rates to consolidate her credit card debt and make repayment more manageable.

Through disciplined budgeting and debt repayment efforts, Emily successfully paid off her credit card debt. She learned valuable financial lessons about the dangers of bad debt and the importance of responsible financial management.

Debt Management Strategies

Effective debt management is essential for individuals seeking to leverage debt strategically and minimize its negative impact. Here are some practical debt management strategies:

1. Prioritize High-Interest Debt: If you have multiple debts, prioritize paying off those with the highest interest rates first. This approach, known as the debt avalanche method, minimizes interest costs and accelerates debt repayment.

2. Create a Debt Repayment Plan: Develop a structured debt repayment plan that outlines how much you will pay toward each debt and when. Having a clear plan helps you stay on track and monitor your progress.

3. Debt Consolidation: Consider consolidating high-interest debt into a lower-interest loan or credit card with a promotional balance transfer rate. This can reduce the overall interest you pay and simplify debt management.

4. Avoid New Debt: While working to pay off existing debt, avoid accumulating new debt, especially high-interest credit card debt. Focus on living within your means and adhering to a budget.

5. Emergency Fund: Maintain an emergency fund to cover unexpected expenses. This prevents you from relying on credit cards or loans to address financial emergencies.

6. Seek Professional Guidance: If you're overwhelmed by debt or unsure about the best debt management strategies for your situation, consult with a financial advisor or credit counselor. They can provide tailored guidance and solutions.

Debt is a financial tool that can either propel individuals toward their wealth-building goals or hold them back. The key to mastering the art of debt management lies in understanding the distinction between good debt and bad debt and using each

130

strategically. Good debt, such as mortgage and student loans, can facilitate asset acquisition and wealth creation, while bad debt, like high-interest credit card balances, can be a financial trap.

By adopting responsible financial practices, prioritizing debt repayment, and seeking professional guidance when needed, individuals can harness the potential of good debt and minimize the negative impact of bad debt. Ultimately, effective debt management is a critical component of achieving financial success and building lasting wealth."

Strategies for Effective Debt Management: Taking Control of Your Financial Future

Debt is a financial tool that, when managed effectively, can help individuals achieve their goals and aspirations. However, when mismanaged, debt can become a heavy burden that impedes financial progress and stifles wealth-building efforts. To regain control of your financial future and set a course towards prosperity, it's essential to implement strategies for effective debt management. In this chapter, we will explore these strategies in detail, providing you with the knowledge and tools to conquer debt and pave the way to financial stability and wealth accumulation.

1. Debt Evaluation: Know Where You Stand

Effective debt management begins with a clear understanding of your current financial situation. It's crucial to assess your debt comprehensively, taking stock of all outstanding balances, their respective interest rates, and minimum monthly payments. This debt evaluation process serves as the foundation for developing a strategic plan to tackle your financial liabilities.

Start by creating a list of all your debts, which may include:

131

- Credit card balances
- Personal loans
- Student loans
- Auto loans
- Mortgage loans
- Medical bills
- Any other outstanding debts

For each debt, gather the following information:

- Principal balance (the initial amount borrowed)
- Interest rate (the annual percentage rate or APR)
- Minimum monthly payment

Organize this information in a clear and easily accessible format, such as a spreadsheet or a dedicated notebook. Having a comprehensive overview of your debts empowers you to make informed decisions and prioritize your repayment strategy.

2. Prioritize High-Interest Debt: The First Battle

Not all debts are created equal. Some come with significantly higher interest rates than others, making them costlier over time. To minimize the financial burden of debt, prioritize tackling high-interest debt as your initial step in debt management.

High-interest debt often takes the form of credit card balances or personal loans with double-digit APRs. These debts not only accumulate interest rapidly but also hinder your ability to make substantial progress in reducing the principal balance when you make only minimum monthly payments.

To address high-interest debt effectively:

- Allocate extra funds, beyond the minimum payments, toward your high-interest debts. This accelerates the reduction of the principal balance and reduces overall interest costs.
- Consider transferring high-interest credit card balances to a lower-interest card or a balance transfer credit card. Balance transfers often come with promotional periods of 0% APR, which can significantly reduce interest costs.
- If possible, explore opportunities to negotiate lower interest rates with your creditors. A lower interest rate means that a larger portion of your payments goes towards reducing the principal balance.

By prioritizing high-interest debt, you not only save money on interest but also create a sense of accomplishment as you see these debts diminish more quickly.

3. Debt Consolidation: Streamlining Your Financial Obligations

Debt consolidation is a strategic approach to managing multiple debts by combining them into a single, more manageable loan or credit account. This can be particularly useful when dealing with various high-interest debts that make tracking and managing payments complex.

There are several debt consolidation options to consider:

- **Consolidation Loans:** Debt consolidation loans are personal loans used to pay off existing debts. These loans typically come with fixed interest rates and fixed repayment terms. By consolidating your debts into a single loan, you simplify your payment schedule and potentially secure a lower overall interest rate.

- **Balance Transfer Credit Cards:** Some credit cards offer promotional balance transfer rates, often at 0% APR for an introductory period. Transferring high-interest credit card balances to a card with a 0% APR promotion can significantly reduce interest costs during the promotional period. Be sure to read the terms and conditions, as there may be fees associated with balance transfers.

- **Home Equity Loans or Lines of Credit:** If you own a home, you may have the option to use your home equity to consolidate debts. Home equity loans and lines of credit typically offer lower interest rates than unsecured loans, but they come with the risk of losing your home if you default on payments. Exercise caution and ensure you can manage the new debt responsibly.

When considering debt consolidation, it's essential to assess the overall cost, including any fees associated with the consolidation method. Additionally, focus on improving financial habits to avoid accumulating new debt after consolidation.

4. Create a Debt Repayment Plan: The Roadmap to Freedom

A well-structured debt repayment plan is your roadmap to financial freedom. It provides a clear path for systematically paying down your debts, tracking your progress, and ultimately achieving debt-free status. Here are the key steps to creating an effective debt repayment plan:

- **List All Debts:** Start by listing all your debts, including their respective interest rates and minimum monthly payments, as you did during the initial debt evaluation.

- **Set Clear Goals:** Define your debt repayment goals. Specify the amount of debt you aim to eliminate and the timeframe within which you plan to achieve this goal.

- **Prioritize Debts:** Decide on your preferred debt repayment strategy. Two common approaches are the "snowball method" and the "avalanche method."

  - The **Snowball Method:** In this strategy, you focus on paying off the smallest debt first while making minimum payments on larger debts. This approach provides a psychological boost by allowing you to experience quick wins, motivating you to continue your debt repayment journey.

- The **Avalanche Method:** The avalanche method, on the other hand, prioritizes paying off the debt with the highest interest rate first, while maintaining minimum payments on other debts. This approach minimizes overall interest costs, potentially leading to faster debt elimination.

Select the strategy that resonates most with your financial personality and preferences. Both methods are effective, and the choice ultimately depends on your priorities and motivations.

- **Allocate a Debt Repayment Budget:** Devote a portion of your monthly budget to debt repayment. Determine how much you can comfortably allocate to pay down your debts while covering essential expenses and building savings.

- **Stick to Your Plan:** Consistency is key to debt reduction. Commit to following your repayment plan diligently. Make the required payments on time and avoid accumulating new debt.

- **Track Your Progress:** Regularly monitor your progress toward your debt repayment goals. Celebrate milestones along the way to maintain motivation and momentum.

- **Adjust as Needed:** Life circumstances can change, affecting your ability to adhere to your original plan. Be flexible and

135

willing to adjust your strategy if necessary, while keeping your ultimate debt-free goal in sight.

Creating a debt repayment plan not only helps you organize your financial obligations but also instills a sense of control and discipline in your financial life. As you witness your debts shrinking, you'll experience a growing sense of empowerment and financial freedom.

5. Lifestyle Adjustment: Temporarily Cut Non-Essentials

To accelerate your debt repayment journey, consider making temporary adjustments to your lifestyle. This may involve cutting non-essential expenses and reallocating those funds toward debt reduction. While it can be challenging to change spending habits, these adjustments can significantly impact your ability to pay off debt faster. Here are some practical steps:

- **Budget Review:** Conduct a thorough review of your budget to identify discretionary expenses that can be reduced or eliminated. Common areas to cut back on include dining out, entertainment, subscription services, and impulse purchases.

- **Frugal Living:** Embrace a frugal lifestyle by seeking ways to save on everyday expenses. Look for discounts, coupons, and promotional offers when shopping for necessities.

- **Minimalism:** Explore minimalism as a way to simplify your life and reduce spending. Selling or donating items you no longer need not only declutters your space but can also generate extra cash to put toward debt.

- **Alternative Transportation:** Consider using public transportation, carpooling, or biking instead of relying solely on your car. This can reduce fuel and maintenance costs.

- **Dining In:** Prepare meals at home instead of dining out. Cooking your own meals is not only cost-effective but also allows you to make healthier choices.

- **Reduce Utility Costs:** Identify opportunities to lower utility bills by being mindful of energy consumption. Simple steps like turning off lights when not in use, adjusting thermostats, and sealing drafts can make a significant difference.

- **Evaluate Subscriptions:** Review your subscriptions, including streaming services, gym memberships, and magazines. Cancel or pause those that you don't regularly use.

By making these lifestyle adjustments, you can redirect funds toward debt repayment without compromising your quality of life. Remember that these changes are temporary and are aimed at helping you achieve your financial goals more quickly.

6. Snowball vs. Avalanche Method: Choose Your Approach

One of the key decisions when creating your debt repayment plan is choosing between the snowball method and the avalanche method. Each has its advantages, and the choice largely depends on your financial priorities and motivations.

The Snowball Method:

In the snowball method, you focus on paying off your smallest debt first while continuing to make minimum payments on your larger debts. This approach provides quick wins, as you eliminate smaller debts sooner, giving you a sense of accomplishment and motivation to keep going. Here's how it works:

1. **List Your Debts:** Start by listing all your debts from smallest to largest based on the outstanding balance.

137

2. **Allocate Extra Payments:** Allocate any extra funds available in your budget to pay off the smallest debt while continuing to make minimum payments on the others.

3. **Snowball Effect:** As you pay off the smallest debt, the amount you were paying toward it becomes available to put toward the next smallest debt. This creates a snowball effect, with the payments growing larger as each debt is eliminated.

4. **Repeat:** Continue this process until you've paid off all your debts.

The snowball method is particularly effective for individuals who find motivation in quick wins and visible progress. It can help build momentum and confidence as you work toward becoming debt-free.

The Avalanche Method:

The avalanche method prioritizes paying off the debt with the highest interest rate first, while maintaining minimum payments on the others. This approach minimizes the overall interest costs of your debts, potentially allowing you to become debt-free more quickly. Here's how it works:

1. **List Your Debts:** Start by listing all your debts, but this time, order them from the highest to the lowest interest rate.

2. **Allocate Extra Payments:** Allocate any extra funds available in your budget to pay off the debt with the highest interest rate, while making minimum payments on the debts with lower interest rates.

3. **Interest Cost Savings:** By targeting the highest interest rate debt first, you reduce the overall interest costs you'll incur

during your debt repayment journey. This approach can potentially save you more money in the long run.

4. **Repeat:** Once the highest interest rate debt is paid off, apply the same strategy to the debt with the next highest interest rate, and continue until you've eliminated all your debts.

The avalanche method is advantageous for those who prioritize minimizing the total interest paid over the course of debt repayment. It may take longer to experience a tangible payoff compared to the snowball method, but the financial savings can be substantial.

Ultimately, the choice between the snowball and avalanche methods depends on your personal financial goals and the psychological factors that motivate you. Some individuals prefer the emotional boost of quick victories provided by the snowball method, while others prioritize the financial benefits of the avalanche method. Whichever approach you select, the key is to stick to your chosen strategy and remain committed to becoming debt-free.

7. Avoid New Debt: Breaking the Cycle

Effectively managing existing debt is a significant step toward financial stability, but it's equally important to prevent the accumulation of new debt. Responsible spending habits are essential to break the cycle of debt and ensure long-term financial success. Here are some strategies to avoid accumulating new debt:

- **Budget Wisely:** Maintain a budget that aligns with your financial goals and helps you track income and expenses. Regularly review your budget to ensure it accommodates necessary expenses while leaving room for savings and debt reduction.

139

- **Emergency Fund:** Build and maintain an emergency fund to cover unexpected expenses or financial setbacks. Having this financial cushion reduces the need to rely on credit cards or loans in times of crisis.

- **Mindful Spending:** Practice mindful spending by distinguishing between needs and wants. Before making a purchase, consider whether it's a necessary expense or a discretionary one. Delay or avoid non-essential purchases whenever possible.

- **Debit Over Credit:** Prefer using debit cards or cash for transactions instead of credit cards. This approach ensures that you're spending money you actually have rather than accumulating debt.

- **Resist Impulse Buying:** Before making impulse purchases, take a moment to evaluate whether the item is a genuine need or a fleeting desire. Delaying gratification can prevent unnecessary spending.

- **Live Below Your Means:** Strive to live below your means by maintaining a lifestyle that allows you to save and invest for the future. Avoid the temptation to increase your spending as your income rises.

- **Regular Financial Check-Ins:** Periodically review your financial goals, budget, and progress toward debt reduction. This helps you stay on track and make necessary adjustments to your financial plan.

- **Credit Card Management:** If you use credit cards, do so responsibly. Pay your credit card balances in full each month to avoid interest charges. Limit the number of credit cards you have to reduce the temptation to accumulate excessive debt.

By adopting these strategies and developing responsible financial habits, you can not only manage your existing debt effectively but also prevent the recurrence of financial challenges in the future. Breaking free from the cycle of debt is a crucial step toward achieving financial stability and securing your financial future.

Effective debt management is a fundamental component of financial success. To take control of your financial future and pave the way to wealth accumulation, consider the following key strategies:

1. **Debt Evaluation:** Begin by assessing your current debt situation, including all outstanding balances, interest rates, and minimum payments.

2. **Prioritize High-Interest Debt:** Focus on tackling high-interest debt first to reduce overall interest costs and accelerate debt reduction.

3. **Debt Consolidation:** Explore debt consolidation options, such as consolidation loans or balance transfers, to streamline your financial obligations and potentially lower interest rates.

4. **Create a Debt Repayment Plan:** Develop a clear debt repayment plan that outlines your goals, prioritizes your debts, and allocates a portion of your budget to debt reduction.

5. **Lifestyle Adjustment:** Temporarily adjust your lifestyle by cutting non-essential expenses and reallocating those funds toward debt repayment.

6. **Choose Your Repayment Method:** Decide between the snowball method, which prioritizes the smallest debts first, or the avalanche method, which focuses on the highest interest rate debts.

7. **Avoid New Debt:** Practice responsible spending habits to prevent the accumulation of new debt and maintain financial stability.

By implementing these strategies and remaining committed to your financial goals, you can regain control of your financial future, eliminate debt, and set a course toward wealth accumulation and financial prosperity. Remember that financial success is not only about managing your existing resources but also about making informed decisions that benefit your long-term financial well-being.

Financial Independence Through Debt Management

Financial independence is a dream that many aspire to achieve. It represents the point at which your financial resources and investments generate enough income to cover your living expenses, allowing you to have the freedom to make choices based on your values and passions, rather than financial constraints. It signifies a life where you are no longer beholden to a traditional job or financial obligations. To embark on the journey to financial independence, effective debt management is a crucial cornerstone.

In this chapter, we will explore how financial independence can be attained through prudent debt management strategies. We'll delve into the principles that underpin this concept and provide actionable steps to set you on the path to financial freedom.

1. Living Below Your Means: The Foundation of Financial Independence

Financial independence starts with a fundamental principle: living below your means. In essence, this means spending less than you earn and consistently saving and investing the difference. The

142

surplus between your income and expenses is what enables you to accumulate wealth over time.

The importance of living below your means cannot be overstated. It sets the stage for sound financial decision-making and is a prerequisite for building a robust financial foundation. To live below your means effectively:

- **Create a Budget:** Begin by creating a comprehensive budget that tracks your income and expenses. Your budget should account for all your financial obligations, including housing, utilities, groceries, transportation, and debt payments. Be meticulous in documenting every expense, no matter how small.

- **Distinguish Between Needs and Wants:** Differentiate between essential needs and discretionary wants. Prioritize spending on necessities, such as housing, food, utilities, and healthcare, while exercising prudence with non-essential expenditures.

- **Cut Unnecessary Expenses:** Identify areas where you can reduce or eliminate unnecessary expenses. This could involve canceling unused subscriptions, dining out less frequently, or finding cost-effective alternatives for common purchases.

- **Set Financial Goals:** Establish clear financial goals that reflect your aspirations and values. Having defined objectives provides motivation and direction for your financial journey.

- **Regularly Review and Adjust:** Periodically review your budget to ensure that it aligns with your goals and current financial circumstances. Adjust your spending habits and financial priorities as needed to stay on course.

Living below your means not only frees up resources for saving and investing but also instills financial discipline. It allows you to accumulate capital that can be channeled into income-generating assets, ultimately accelerating your journey to financial independence.

2. Building an Emergency Fund: A Safety Net for Financial Independence

Financial independence is built on a foundation of financial security. An essential component of this security is the presence of an emergency fund. An emergency fund is a dedicated savings account designed to cover unexpected expenses or financial setbacks without resorting to taking on additional debt.

The importance of an emergency fund cannot be overstated. It provides a financial safety net that allows you to weather unforeseen circumstances, such as medical emergencies, car repairs, or unexpected job loss, without derailing your progress toward financial independence.

Here's how to establish and manage an effective emergency fund:

- **Determine Your Target:** Aim to save at least three to six months' worth of living expenses in your emergency fund. The exact amount will depend on your personal circumstances and risk tolerance. Individuals with more volatile income sources may benefit from a larger emergency fund.

- **Open a Separate Account:** To avoid the temptation of dipping into your emergency fund for non-emergencies, open a separate savings account specifically designated for this purpose. Ensure that the account is easily accessible in case of urgent need.

- **Regular Contributions:** Consistently contribute to your emergency fund as part of your budgeting process. Automate transfers from your primary checking account to your emergency fund account to ensure regular savings.

- **Use for Genuine Emergencies:** Reserve your emergency fund exclusively for genuine emergencies, such as medical expenses, unexpected home repairs, or temporary job loss. Avoid using it for discretionary spending or non-urgent financial goals.

- **Replenish After Use:** If you need to tap into your emergency fund, make it a priority to replenish the withdrawn amount as soon as your financial situation allows. Rebuilding your emergency fund ensures that it remains a reliable safety net.

Having a well-funded emergency fund provides peace of mind, reduces financial stress, and safeguards your progress toward financial independence. It allows you to navigate unexpected challenges without compromising your long-term financial goals.

3. Automate Savings and Investments: Consistency is Key

Achieving financial independence is a long-term endeavor that requires consistent effort and discipline. One effective strategy to ensure regular savings and investments is automation. Automation simplifies the process of setting aside money for your future financial goals, making it a seamless and routine part of your financial life.

Automating your savings and investments offers several advantages:

- **Consistency:** Automation ensures that you consistently contribute to your savings and investment accounts. Regular contributions, even if they are modest, can accumulate significantly over time.

- **Discipline:** It eliminates the need for manual transfers or decision-making, reducing the temptation to spend rather than save. Automation enforces financial discipline.

- **Time Efficiency:** Setting up automated transfers takes only a few minutes, saving you the time and effort required for manual contributions.

- **Reduced Procrastination:** Automation minimizes the risk of procrastination or forgetting to save or invest. Once it's set up, it operates without your direct involvement.

To get started with automating your savings and investments, follow these steps:

- **Identify Your Financial Goals:** Begin by identifying your financial goals. Determine what you're saving or investing for, whether it's retirement, a down payment on a home, an emergency fund, or other objectives.

- **Choose the Right Accounts:** Select the appropriate savings or investment accounts for each of your goals. This might include a high-yield savings account, an individual retirement account (IRA), a 401(k), or a brokerage account, depending on your goals and investment horizon.

- **Set Up Automatic Transfers:** Contact your bank or financial institution to set up automatic transfers from your primary checking account to your designated savings or investment accounts. You'll specify the frequency and amount of the transfers.

- **Coordinate with Payroll:** If you have access to employer-sponsored retirement accounts, such as a 401(k), coordinate with your HR department to automate contributions directly from your paycheck. Employer matches and pre-tax contributions can provide additional benefits.

- **Monitor and Adjust:** Regularly monitor your automated contributions to ensure they align with your financial goals and circumstances. Adjust the amounts as your income or financial objectives change.

Automation is a powerful tool for achieving financial independence because it establishes a consistent savings habit. Over time, the compounding effect of your regular contributions can lead to substantial wealth accumulation.

4. Multiple Income Streams: Diversifying Your Financial Resources

One of the fundamental principles of financial independence is diversification, not only in your investments but also in your income sources. Relying solely on one source of income, such as your job, leaves you vulnerable to economic fluctuations and unexpected events. Diversifying your income streams enhances your financial security and accelerates your journey to financial independence.

Here are several strategies for diversifying your income sources:

- **Side Hustles:** Explore side hustles or part-time work that align with your skills and interests. Side gigs can supplement your primary income and provide additional financial stability.

- **Investment Income:** Invest in income-generating assets such as dividend stocks, bonds, or real estate. The income generated from these investments can contribute to your financial security and independence.

- **Passive Income:** Passive income streams, such as rental income from real estate or royalties from intellectual property, can provide consistent income with minimal active involvement.

- **Entrepreneurship:** Consider starting a small business or investing in entrepreneurial ventures. Entrepreneurship can offer the potential for unlimited income, but it often involves more significant risks and responsibilities.

- **Online Income Opportunities:** Leverage the digital economy to generate income through various online opportunities, including affiliate marketing, e-commerce, freelance work, and content creation.

- **Diversify Your Investments:** Diversification isn't limited to income sources; it also applies to your investments. Build a diversified portfolio that includes a mix of asset classes, such as stocks, bonds, and real estate.

Diversifying your income sources reduces your reliance on a single paycheck and enhances your financial resilience. Multiple income streams provide a safety net, ensuring that you have alternative sources of funds to cover expenses or invest for the future.

5. Retirement Planning: Securing Your Financial Future

A core element of achieving financial independence is diligent retirement planning. Retirement planning involves systematically saving and investing to build a financial nest egg that will sustain you in your post-working years. While financial independence can provide the freedom to retire early, traditional retirement planning remains essential for securing your financial future.

Here are key steps to effective retirement planning:

- **Start Early:** The earlier you begin saving for retirement, the more time your investments have to grow. Start as soon as possible, even if you can only contribute a small amount initially.

148

- **Utilize Retirement Accounts:** Take advantage of employer-sponsored retirement accounts like 401(k)s or similar plans. These accounts offer tax advantages and, in many cases, employer matching contributions.

- **Contribute Regularly:** Commit to regular contributions to your retirement accounts. Automate these contributions to ensure consistency.

- **Diversify Your Investments:** Build a diversified retirement portfolio that aligns with your risk tolerance and retirement timeline. This typically includes a mix of stocks, bonds, and other assets.

- **Review and Adjust:** Periodically review your retirement plan to assess your progress and adjust your contributions or investment strategy as needed. Life circumstances, market conditions, and retirement goals can change over time.

- **Consult a Financial Advisor:** Seek guidance from a financial advisor or retirement specialist, especially as you approach retirement age. They can help you make informed decisions regarding asset allocation, withdrawal strategies, and tax-efficient retirement planning.

- **Consider Early Retirement:** If early retirement is a goal, develop a detailed plan that accounts for how you will cover living expenses and healthcare costs before reaching the typical retirement age. This may involve additional savings or alternative income sources.

- **Plan for Healthcare:** Healthcare expenses can be a significant portion of retirement costs. Explore options for healthcare coverage, including Medicare, and factor these expenses into your retirement budget.

149

Retirement planning is essential for securing your financial future and achieving long-term financial independence. It ensures that you have the resources to maintain your desired lifestyle and enjoy the freedom of retirement on your terms.

Achieving financial independence is a profound and attainable goal that requires a deliberate and disciplined approach to debt management, living below your means, building a robust emergency fund, automating savings and investments, diversifying your income sources, and diligent retirement planning. Financial independence represents a life where your financial resources work for you, providing the freedom to pursue your passions, make choices aligned with your values, and enjoy peace of mind about your financial future. By following the principles and strategies outlined in this chapter, you can embark on a transformative journey toward financial independence and wealth mastery.

Living a Fulfilling Life Below Your Means

Living below your means is often seen as a pathway to financial security and wealth accumulation, but it's not just about accumulating money; it's about living a fulfilling and intentional life. This chapter explores the art of living below your means while maximizing happiness, fulfillment, and aligning your spending with your values and long-term goals.

1. Value-Based Spending: Prioritizing What Matters

At the heart of living below your means while leading a fulfilling life is value-based spending. This approach encourages you to identify and prioritize the things that matter most to you. By aligning your spending with your core values, you can derive greater satisfaction from your financial choices.

Here's how to implement value-based spending:

Identify Your Core Values: Begin by reflecting on your values. What is most important to you in life? It could be family, health, personal growth, community, adventure, or any number of other values. Make a list of your top values.

Link Spending to Values: Review your spending habits and assess whether they align with your values. Are you spending money on things that truly matter to you? For example, if family is a core value, are you allocating resources for quality time and experiences with loved ones?

Prioritize Meaningful Expenses: Once you've identified your core values, prioritize expenses that contribute to those values. If adventure is a priority, allocate resources for travel experiences. If community is essential, invest in social gatherings and activities that strengthen your connections.

Cut Back on Non-Essentials: On the flip side, consider cutting back on expenses that don't align with your values. These are often the discretionary expenses that bring limited joy or fulfillment. Reducing or eliminating them can free up resources for what truly matters.

Value-based spending encourages a mindful approach to financial decisions, ensuring that your money serves as a tool for enhancing your life in meaningful ways.

2. Mindful Consumption: The Power of Intentional Spending

Mindful consumption is a practice that involves intentional and thoughtful spending. It's about being present and aware when making purchasing decisions, considering the impact of those choices on your life and well-being. Here's how to incorporate mindful consumption into your life:

Pause and Reflect: Before making a purchase, take a moment to pause and reflect. Ask yourself if this purchase aligns with your values and contributes positively to your life. Consider whether it's a need or a want.

Question Impulse Purchases: Impulse buying is a common habit that can lead to overspending and clutter. Challenge yourself to resist impulse purchases by waiting 24 hours before buying something non-essential. This delay can help you make more considered choices.

Practice Gratitude: Cultivate gratitude for what you already have. Regularly reflect on the abundance in your life, which can reduce the desire for unnecessary acquisitions. A gratitude practice can also boost overall happiness.

Quality Over Quantity: Favor quality over quantity when it comes to purchases. Invest in items or experiences that offer long-lasting value and utility. This approach can reduce waste and save money in the long run.

**Mindful consumption is about savoring the present moment and finding contentment in what you already possess. It allows you to avoid the trap of consumerism and appreciate the abundance in your life.

3. Minimalism: Less Is More

Minimalism is a lifestyle and philosophy that emphasizes simplicity and the intentional reduction of possessions and distractions. It's about focusing on what truly matters and eliminating the excess that can clutter your life and finances.

Here are some principles of minimalism and how they relate to living below your means:

Declutter Your Life: Minimalism encourages decluttering your physical and mental space. By letting go of possessions, obligations, or commitments that no longer serve you, you free up resources for what's essential.

Prioritize Experiences: Minimalism emphasizes experiences over material possessions. Instead of accumulating more stuff, invest in experiences and moments that bring joy and fulfillment.

Quality Over Quantity: As a minimalist, you prioritize quality over quantity. This applies to your possessions, relationships, and experiences. Invest in high-quality items that last longer and provide more value.

Reduce Financial Stress: Living a minimalist lifestyle can reduce financial stress. By simplifying your financial commitments and avoiding unnecessary expenses, you can live comfortably on less.

Minimalism isn't about depriving yourself but rather about focusing on the meaningful and purposeful aspects of life. By adopting a minimalist mindset, you can embrace living below your means as a deliberate choice to prioritize what truly matters.

4. Frugality: Maximizing Value, Minimizing Waste

Frugality is a practice of resourcefulness and cost-consciousness. It involves finding ways to maximize value and minimize waste in your daily life. Frugality isn't about being cheap; it's about being efficient with your resources.

Here are some strategies for embracing frugality while living a fulfilling life:

Budgeting: Create a budget that outlines your income and expenses. This helps you track where your money is going and identify areas where you can cut costs.

Smart Shopping: Practice smart shopping by looking for deals, using coupons, and comparing prices before making purchases. Avoid buying on impulse and opt for value-based choices.

Reduce, Reuse, Recycle: Adopt a sustainable mindset by reducing waste, reusing items when possible, and recycling materials. Reducing waste can also save you money on disposable products.

DIY and Self-Sufficiency: Embrace a do-it-yourself (DIY) mentality by learning to perform tasks or make items yourself. Whether it's gardening, home repairs, or crafting, DIY efforts can save you money and provide a sense of accomplishment.

Frugal Entertainment: Seek out affordable or free entertainment options in your community, such as parks, libraries, community events, and free cultural activities. Enjoying cost-effective leisure can be just as satisfying as expensive entertainment.

Minimalism and Frugality: Minimalism and frugality often go hand in hand. Minimalism encourages you to eliminate the excess in your life, while frugality helps you make the most of what you have. Combining these principles can lead to a more intentional and resourceful lifestyle.

By embracing frugality, you can reduce your expenses and increase your savings, all while maintaining a fulfilling and satisfying life.

Living Below Your Means: A Fulfilling Journey

Living below your means isn't a one-size-fits-all approach. It's a dynamic and personal journey that evolves as your financial situation and life circumstances change. By incorporating value-based spending, mindful consumption, minimalism, and frugality into your lifestyle, you can achieve the dual goals of financial security and personal fulfillment.

Remember that the ultimate aim of living below your means is to create a life that aligns with your values and aspirations. It's about optimizing your resources to maximize happiness, contentment, and well-being. While it may involve making adjustments and conscious choices, the rewards of this journey extend far beyond financial gain. They encompass a sense of freedom, purpose, and peace that money alone cannot buy.

Financial Independence: The Ultimate Goal

Living below your means is a fundamental step toward achieving financial independence. Financial independence is a state where you have accumulated enough wealth and passive income to cover your living expenses, allowing you to work by choice rather than necessity. It provides you with the freedom to pursue your passions, travel, spend time with loved ones, or engage in activities that bring you joy.

Here are essential principles and strategies for attaining financial independence through effective money management:

1. Living Below Your Means: As discussed, living below your means is the foundation of financial independence. It enables you to save and invest a significant portion of your income, accelerating your journey toward financial freedom.

2. Building an Emergency Fund: Financial independence requires a safety net. An emergency fund is a crucial component

155

of this safety net, providing a financial cushion to cover unexpected expenses or income disruptions.

3. Automate Savings and Investments: Automating your savings and investments ensures consistency and discipline. Set up automatic transfers to your savings and retirement accounts, making it a habit to allocate a portion of your income toward future financial security.

4. Multiple Income Streams: Diversify your income sources to reduce reliance on a single paycheck. Multiple income streams can include a combination of earned income, passive income, and portfolio income.

5. Retirement Planning: Secure your future by actively contributing to retirement accounts such as 401(k)s or IRAs. Take advantage of employer matches and seek professional guidance for retirement planning.

6. Frugality and Mindful Spending: Continuously practice frugality and mindful spending to maximize the efficiency of your financial resources. By reducing waste and making thoughtful spending choices, you can divert more money toward savings and investments.

7. Debt Management: Effectively manage and reduce debt to free up more of your income for saving and investing. Prioritize high-interest debt and consider debt consolidation strategies.

8. Investment Strategy: Develop a diversified and long-term investment strategy that aligns with your financial goals. Consider a mix of stocks, bonds, real estate, and other assets to optimize returns and manage risk.

9. Passive Income: Strive to build sources of passive income, such as rental properties, dividend-paying stocks, or royalty income. Passive income can provide financial stability and contribute to your journey to financial independence.

10. Financial Education: Invest in your financial education to make informed decisions about investments, taxes, and financial planning. Knowledge is a valuable asset on the path to financial independence.

11. Evaluate and Adjust: Regularly review your financial progress and make necessary adjustments. Life circumstances, market conditions, and personal goals can change, necessitating revisions to your financial plan.

Financial Independence: A Personal Journey

Financial independence is not a one-size-fits-all goal. It's a highly personal journey that depends on your individual circumstances, aspirations, and timeline. Some individuals may achieve financial independence in their 30s, while others may do so in their 50s or beyond. What matters most is the commitment to the journey and the progress you make along the way.

Living Below Your Means and Quality of Life

It's essential to recognize that living below your means doesn't equate to living a deprived or joyless life. On the contrary, it's a deliberate choice to enhance your quality of life by aligning your spending with your values and long-term goals. Here's how:

Peace of Mind: Financial stress can take a toll on your well-being. Living below your means reduces financial stress, providing peace of mind and emotional stability.

Freedom and Flexibility: By spending intentionally and saving consistently, you gain the freedom to make choices based on your desires rather than financial constraints. Whether it's taking a sabbatical, starting a new venture, or traveling the world, financial independence offers flexibility.

Reduced Pressure: Living within your means means you're less likely to rely on credit, loans, or high-pressure financial decisions. This reduces the pressure to accumulate debt or engage in risky financial behaviors.

Investing in Experiences: Value-based spending encourages you to invest in experiences and moments rather than material possessions. These experiences often lead to lasting memories and personal growth, enriching your life in meaningful ways. Travel, cultural exploration, educational pursuits, and quality time with loved ones become more accessible and enjoyable.

Savings as a Tool for Achieving Dreams: Savings aren't just numbers in a bank account; they are the stepping stones to realizing your dreams. Whether your aspirations involve homeownership, starting a business, supporting a cause, or early retirement, savings provide the means to turn those dreams into reality.

Balancing the Present and Future: Living below your means strikes a balance between enjoying the present and preparing for the future. While it's essential to appreciate today's experiences, it's equally important to secure your financial future and ensure you can continue to enjoy life's pleasures.

Resilience in Times of Uncertainty: Financial independence and living below your means provide resilience during uncertain times. Having a financial buffer and diversified income streams can help you weather unexpected events, economic downturns, or personal challenges with greater ease.

Impact on Relationships: Sharing financial values and goals with a partner or family members can enhance relationships.

When you're aligned in your approach to money and resources, it fosters a sense of teamwork and shared purpose.

A Mindful and Intentional Life: Ultimately, living below your means cultivates a mindful and intentional life. It encourages you to question societal norms and consumerism, empowering you to make choices that genuinely resonate with your values.

The Journey to Financial Independence: Your Personal Roadmap

Your journey to financial independence is a marathon, not a sprint. It requires discipline, patience, and adaptability. While there are overarching principles and strategies, your path will be unique to your circumstances and desires.

Consider the following steps as you embark on your journey to financial independence:

1. Define Your Financial Goals: Clearly articulate your short-term and long-term financial goals. These could include building an emergency fund, paying off debt, buying a home, saving for education, or achieving early retirement.

2. Create a Financial Plan: Develop a comprehensive financial plan that outlines how you will reach your goals. Your plan should include a budget, debt reduction strategy, savings targets, investment strategies, and a timeline for achieving milestones.

3. Prioritize Saving and Investing: Allocate a significant portion of your income to savings and investments. Automate contributions to ensure consistency.

4. Monitor Your Progress: Regularly review your financial plan and assess your progress toward your goals. Adjust your plan as needed to account for changes in income, expenses, or financial priorities.

5. Seek Professional Guidance: Consider working with financial advisors or professionals, especially for complex financial matters like investment portfolio management, tax planning, or estate planning.

6. Embrace Lifelong Learning: Continuously educate yourself about personal finance, investments, and wealth-building strategies. Financial literacy is a powerful tool on your journey to financial independence.

7. Cultivate Patience: Achieving financial independence takes time and dedication. Understand that there may be challenges and setbacks along the way, but persistence is key.

8. Celebrate Milestones: Acknowledge and celebrate your financial milestones, both big and small. Recognizing your progress can provide motivation and a sense of accomplishment.

9. Share Your Journey: Consider sharing your financial journey with loved ones or joining a supportive community of like-minded individuals. Sharing experiences and insights can be inspiring and help you stay on track.

10. Embrace a Mindful Lifestyle: As you work toward financial independence, embrace mindful living. Focus on value-based spending, mindful consumption, minimalism, and frugality to ensure that your choices align with your values and aspirations.

Closer together

Living below your means is not a one-time decision; it's a continuous lifestyle choice that leads to financial security, wealth accumulation, and personal fulfillment. It's a journey that involves thoughtful spending, prudent saving, wise investing, and a commitment to aligning your financial choices with your values and goals.

Remember that the pursuit of financial independence is not solely about accumulating wealth but about enhancing the quality of your life. It's a journey that empowers you to make choices that truly matter to you, to create lasting memories, and to secure a future that aligns with your dreams.

As you embark on this journey, be patient, stay focused on your goals, and embrace the principles and strategies discussed in this book. By doing so, you can chart a course toward a life of financial freedom, purpose, and contentment, where you not only live below your means but also thrive within them.

Case Study 1: Debt-Free and Thriving

Emily's journey to financial independence began with a decision to take control of her financial situation. Fresh out of college, she found herself burdened with student loans and credit card debt. It was a common predicament for many recent graduates, but Emily was determined to change her financial trajectory.

The Debt Challenge:

Emily's first step was to confront her debt head-on. She gathered all her financial statements and created a detailed list of her outstanding debts, including the principal balances, interest rates, and minimum monthly payments. Seeing the numbers on paper was a wake-up call. She knew that if she continued making only minimum payments, she'd be stuck in debt for years.

The Frugal Lifestyle:

161

To accelerate her debt payoff, Emily adopted a frugal lifestyle. She meticulously analyzed her spending habits, identifying areas where she could cut back without sacrificing her well-being. She started cooking meals at home, canceled unnecessary subscriptions, and limited discretionary spending.

Emily made a budget that allowed her to allocate a significant portion of her income to debt repayment while still covering essential expenses. This disciplined approach was challenging at times, but Emily remained focused on her goal of becoming debt-free.

The Debt Snowball Method:

Emily chose the debt snowball method to tackle her debt. She listed her debts from smallest to largest and focused on paying off the smallest one first, while making minimum payments on the others. This approach provided psychological motivation as she saw her smaller debts disappear quickly.

As each debt was paid off, Emily redirected the money that had been going toward it to the next smallest debt. This snowball effect accelerated her debt repayment progress. It wasn't long before she celebrated paying off her first credit card balance. The sense of accomplishment spurred her on.

Redirecting Debt Payments:

With her credit card debt eliminated, Emily had additional cash flow that was no longer tied up in debt payments. She immediately put this newfound financial freedom to work. Instead of increasing her spending, she began allocating those funds toward savings and investments.

Emily opened a high-yield savings account and automated regular contributions to it. This became her emergency fund, providing a financial safety net for unexpected expenses. Knowing she had savings in place gave her peace of mind and reduced financial stress.

Investing for the Future:

As her student loan balances continued to shrink, Emily started exploring investment options. She educated herself about stocks, bonds, and retirement accounts. She realized that investing was a crucial part of her journey to financial independence.

Emily opened an Individual Retirement Account (IRA) and began contributing consistently. She also diversified her investment portfolio by purchasing a mix of stocks and bonds. With every investment, she saw herself inching closer to her long-term goal of financial freedom.

Achieving Financial Independence:

Over time, Emily paid off her student loans and all other debts. She continued to live frugally, making conscious choices about her spending. By redirecting the money that used to go toward debt payments into savings and investments, she built a substantial nest egg.

Her disciplined approach to managing debt and her commitment to financial responsibility had paid off. Emily achieved financial independence, which meant that she had enough savings and investments to cover her living expenses without relying on traditional employment.

Living Her Dreams:

Emily's journey didn't end with financial independence; it was just the beginning of a new chapter in her life. She realized that true wealth wasn't just about money; it was about having the freedom to pursue her passions and dreams.

Emily used her newfound financial freedom to travel the world, volunteer for causes she cared about, and explore entrepreneurial opportunities. She had the flexibility to design her life on her terms, knowing that her financial foundation was solid.

Emily's story serves as a powerful example of how disciplined debt management, frugal living, and smart financial choices can lead to financial independence and the ability to live a life filled with purpose and fulfillment.

Case Study 2: From Financial Struggles to Freedom

James had always been a hardworking individual, but life threw him some curveballs that led to significant financial challenges. Despite facing adversity, he embarked on a journey to regain control of his financial destiny and achieve financial independence.

The Debt Challenge:

James' financial struggles began when he lost his job during a period of economic downturn. He was suddenly faced with the reality of unemployment and mounting debt. The bills started piling up, and he found himself unable to meet all his financial obligations.

Instead of succumbing to despair, James decided to confront his debt and take proactive steps to address it. He knew that he needed to regain control over his finances and secure his financial future.

Debt Consolidation and Lifestyle Adjustments:

One of the first strategies James employed was debt consolidation. He combined his high-interest credit card debt into a lower-interest personal loan. This not only reduced the overall interest rate on his debt but also simplified his debt repayment process.

James also made significant lifestyle adjustments. He cut back on non-essential expenses, such as dining out and entertainment. He created a budget that allowed him to allocate a substantial portion of his income toward debt repayment while still covering essential living costs.

Emergency Fund and Financial Stability:

As James diligently chipped away at his debt, he simultaneously focused on building an emergency fund. He recognized the importance of having a financial safety net to cover unexpected expenses or emergencies without resorting to further borrowing.

Over time, James built up his emergency fund, which provided him with a sense of financial security he hadn't felt in years. This fund served as a crucial buffer against life's uncertainties, reducing his financial stress.

Beginning to Invest:

Once James had successfully paid off his high-interest debt and established a more stable financial foundation, he turned his attention to investing for the future. He knew that achieving financial independence required not only eliminating debt but also building wealth over time.

James started by contributing to his employer-sponsored retirement account, taking full advantage of the employer's matching contributions. He also opened a brokerage account to invest in stocks and bonds. He educated himself about investment strategies and diversified his portfolio to manage risk effectively.

Financial Freedom Achieved:

As the years went by, James made consistent progress. He not only paid off all his debt but also continued to invest for the future. His retirement savings grew steadily, and his brokerage account flourished with a diversified portfolio.

James achieved financial independence, a milestone he once thought was out of reach. Financial independence meant that he had accumulated enough wealth to support his desired lifestyle without the need for traditional employment.

Today, James enjoys the freedom to pursue his passions, travel, and spend time with his loved ones. He's no longer burdened by the weight of debt or financial stress. Instead, he's on a path of continued financial growth and fulfillment.

Case Study 3: A Life Aligned with Values

Lisa's journey to financial independence took a unique path—one that prioritized values, mindfulness, and simplicity over material wealth. Her story demonstrates that achieving financial independence isn't solely about accumulating wealth but also about finding contentment and fulfillment in a life aligned with one's values.

Discovering Minimalism:

Lisa's journey began when she stumbled upon the concept of minimalism. She was drawn to the idea of simplifying her life and focusing on what truly mattered to her. Lisa realized that her pursuit of material possessions hadn't brought her the happiness she had hoped for.

Driven by a desire for change, Lisa decided to embrace minimalism as a guiding principle in her life. She started by decluttering her home, letting go of unnecessary possessions, and simplifying her living space. The act of decluttering was liberating and made her feel lighter, both physically and mentally.

Mindful Spending:

As Lisa continued to explore minimalism, she extended it to her approach to spending. She adopted mindful spending practices, which involved considering whether each purchase added genuine value to her life. Lisa became more intentional about her consumption habits and avoided impulse buying.

She also started tracking her expenses to gain a clear understanding of her spending patterns. By doing so, Lisa was able to identify areas where she could further reduce expenses, creating opportunities for saving and investing.

Aligning Spending with Values:

A pivotal moment in Lisa's journey was when she identified her core values. She realized that her happiness and fulfillment were closely tied to her values, which included experiences, relationships, personal growth, and giving back to the community.

With her values clearly defined, Lisa began to align her spending with them. She redirected her financial resources toward experiences that enriched her life, such as travel, education, and meaningful social connections. She also allocated a portion of her income to charitable giving and community involvement.

Building a Sustainable Financial Future:

Lisa's approach to financial independence wasn't solely about saving and investing for the future; it was about creating a sustainable and fulfilling present. She maintained an emergency fund to cover unexpected expenses but avoided accumulating unnecessary wealth for its own sake.

Instead of pursuing traditional retirement planning, Lisa continued to work in a capacity that allowed her to contribute to her community and engage in projects that resonated with her values. Her lifestyle wasn't extravagant, but it was rich in experiences, relationships, and a sense of purpose.

True Contentment and Fulfillment:

Lisa's story serves as a reminder that financial independence isn't a one-size-fits-all concept. It can be achieved through various paths, and the destination can look different for each person. For Lisa, it was about aligning her financial choices with her values, embracing minimalism, and finding true contentment and fulfillment in the present moment.

As she continued her journey, Lisa felt a profound sense of freedom and happiness. She had achieved financial independence not by accumulating excessive wealth, but by living a life that resonated with her deepest values and aspirations.

Let it be told, these case studies illustrate that achieving financial independence is a journey that often involves overcoming challenges, making intentional choices, and aligning one's financial strategies with personal values and goals. Whether through disciplined debt management, smart investing, or minimalist living, the path to financial independence is unique to each individual, but the destination—freedom, fulfillment, and the ability to pursue one's passions—remains a universal aspiration.

The Path to Financial Freedom

Debt management is a critical component of financial freedom and wealth building. By distinguishing between good and bad debt, adopting effective debt management strategies, and living below your means, you can pave the way to financial independence. Remember that financial freedom is not about deprivation; it's about making conscious choices that empower you to live a fulfilling life aligned with your values and aspirations.

Chapter 7: Building Multiple Income Streams

In our ongoing journey toward wealth mastery, one of the most powerful strategies is to create and nurture multiple income streams. This approach not only enhances financial security but also accelerates wealth accumulation. In this chapter, we will explore the concept of building multiple income streams for financial stability and growth. We'll highlight opportunities in the gig economy, side hustles, and investments as avenues for additional income. Additionally, we'll provide real-life case studies of individuals who have successfully diversified their income sources, demonstrating the transformative potential of this approach.

The Power of Diversifying Income

Relying solely on a single source of income, such as a full-time job, can leave you vulnerable to economic fluctuations and unexpected setbacks. Creating multiple income streams diversifies your financial resources and enhances your ability to weather financial storms. Let's explore the benefits of diversifying income:

1. Financial Security: The Power of Multiple Income Streams

Financial security is a universal aspiration. It represents a state of financial stability and preparedness where you have the resources to cover your basic needs, handle unexpected expenses, and even pursue your goals and dreams. One of the most effective ways to enhance your financial security is by creating and maintaining multiple income streams.

When you rely on a single income source, such as a traditional job, you are essentially putting all your financial eggs in one basket. While this might provide a sense of stability, it can also leave you vulnerable to financial hardships if that one income source is disrupted. This could happen due to various reasons, including job loss, economic downturns, or unexpected life events.

Multiple income streams, on the other hand, function as a financial safety net. They offer you the peace of mind that comes from knowing that even if one stream is affected, others can continue to support your financial needs. Let's delve into how multiple income streams contribute to financial security:

a. Resilience in Times of Crisis:

One of the most significant advantages of having multiple income streams is the resilience it provides during challenging times. For instance, if you lose your job unexpectedly, having other sources of income can soften the blow and help you weather the storm without falling into financial turmoil.

Consider the scenario of John, a software engineer who diversified his income streams. In addition to his full-time job, he had a side business as a freelance web developer and had invested in dividend-paying stocks. When his employer downsized during an economic downturn and John's position was eliminated, he faced a job loss. However, his freelance work and dividend income provided him with some financial stability during his job search.

b. Protection Against Income Volatility:

In some professions or industries, income can be highly variable. Commission-based sales jobs, for example, often result in fluctuating income levels. Multiple income streams can help smooth out these income variations, ensuring you have a consistent cash flow to meet your financial obligations.

171

Take the example of Maria, a real estate agent. Real estate income can be unpredictable, with some months yielding substantial commissions and others being lean. To mitigate this volatility, Maria diversified her income streams by investing in rental properties, generating rental income in addition to her real estate commissions. This diversification allowed her to maintain a more stable financial situation, even during slow sales periods.

c. Protection Against Unexpected Expenses:

Life is full of surprises, and many of them come with financial implications. Whether it's a medical emergency, car repair, or home maintenance issue, having multiple income streams means you're better prepared to handle unexpected expenses without resorting to debt or draining your savings.

Sarah, a single mother, understands the importance of this aspect of financial security. In addition to her full-time job, she earns income from a part-time consulting gig and runs a small e-commerce business. When her car unexpectedly needed a major repair, she was relieved that her extra income streams could cover the cost without putting her in a financial bind.

2. Accelerated Wealth Building: The Multiplier Effect of Multiple Income Streams

Building wealth is a key financial goal for many individuals. Wealth accumulation provides the financial resources needed to achieve your dreams, whether they involve early retirement, starting a business, traveling the world, or supporting charitable causes. Multiple income streams can be a powerful accelerator in your journey to wealth building.

a. Increased Savings and Investment Capacity:

One of the fundamental principles of wealth building is to save and invest your money wisely. Having multiple income streams significantly boosts your capacity to save and invest. Each additional stream of income contributes to your financial pool, providing more capital to allocate toward your financial goals.

Let's look at Mark, who pursued multiple income streams to expedite his wealth-building journey. In addition to his primary job, he invested in dividend-paying stocks, generated rental income from an investment property, and ran a successful side business. This diversified income allowed him to save and invest a significant portion of his earnings. Over time, the compounding effect of these investments helped him accumulate wealth at a faster rate than he could have achieved with a single income source.

b. Financial Flexibility:

Having multiple income streams also enhances your financial flexibility. You're better equipped to seize investment opportunities or make strategic financial decisions when you have surplus income from various sources.

Consider the case of Lisa, who embraced multiple income streams to achieve her wealth-building goals. Lisa worked full-time in a corporate job but also had a side hustle as a freelance writer and invested in a diversified portfolio of stocks and bonds. When a unique investment opportunity arose—a chance to invest in a promising startup—Lisa had the financial flexibility to participate. This investment turned out to be highly profitable, significantly boosting her overall wealth.

c. Faster Debt Repayment:

If you have debt, such as student loans, credit card balances, or a mortgage, multiple income streams can help you repay it more

173

rapidly. The additional income can be allocated toward debt reduction, reducing the interest costs and the time it takes to become debt-free. This accelerated debt repayment not only frees up your income but also removes a significant financial burden, allowing you to redirect your resources towards wealth-building endeavors.

Imagine Sarah, a recent graduate with a sizeable student loan. To expedite her journey to financial independence, Sarah decided to create multiple income streams. In addition to her entry-level job, she took on freelance writing projects, started a part-time tutoring business, and monetized her creative hobbies through an online store. The additional income from these streams allowed her to make larger monthly payments towards her student loans, ultimately enabling her to pay off her debt several years ahead of schedule.

3. Increased Financial Independence: Liberating Your Time and Choices

Financial independence is a cherished goal for many individuals. It signifies the ability to make life decisions based on your desires and aspirations rather than being constrained by financial obligations. Multiple income streams can be a catalyst for achieving this coveted state of autonomy and control over your life.

a. Reduced Dependency on Employment:

For most people, traditional employment is a significant income source. While employment can provide financial stability, it often comes with the trade-off of time and limited flexibility. Multiple income streams can help reduce your dependency on a single job, giving you more freedom to explore other opportunities or allocate your time differently.

Take the example of Rachel, a graphic designer who decided to pursue her passion for travel and adventure. While maintaining her full-time job, she also leveraged her design skills to offer freelance services online. As her freelance income grew, she gradually reduced her hours at her job and transitioned into a part-time role. This transition allowed her to have more time for her adventures and experience a greater sense of independence.

b. Quicker Path to Retirement:

For those aiming to retire early or achieve financial independence sooner, multiple income streams can be a game-changer. These additional sources of income can accelerate your savings and investment efforts, potentially enabling you to retire earlier than you originally planned.

Consider the case of Michael, a software developer who yearned for early retirement. In addition to his primary job, Michael invested in dividend-paying stocks and real estate properties, generating rental income. The income from these streams, coupled with his disciplined savings, allowed him to retire comfortably in his early 50s, a decade ahead of the traditional retirement age.

c. Pursuing Passion Projects:

Financial independence means having the freedom to pursue your passions and interests without financial constraints. Multiple income streams can provide you with the financial support to engage in passion projects, whether it's starting a non-profit organization, writing a book, or pursuing a creative endeavor.

Emily, an educator, always dreamed of launching a literacy program for underserved communities. By diversifying her income through investments and additional part-time work, she was able to allocate time and resources to turn her dream into a reality. Her passion project not only enriched her life but also positively impacted her community.

All roads to financial security, accelerated wealth building, and increased financial independence can be significantly smoother and more achievable with multiple income streams. These streams provide a buffer during financial hardships, accelerate your wealth accumulation, and grant you greater autonomy over your life choices. By diversifying your income sources and managing them effectively, you can unlock the full potential of your financial journey and experience a more secure and fulfilling life.

In the next section, we will explore the practical steps and strategies to create and manage multiple income streams effectively, providing you with actionable guidance to embark on your journey toward financial security and independence.

Exploring Income Diversity

Diversifying income sources can take various forms, depending on your skills, interests, and resources. Here are some avenues to consider:
1. The Gig Economy: Exploring Flexible Work Opportunities

The gig economy has experienced rapid growth in recent years, transforming the way people work and earn income. It's characterized by short-term contracts, freelance assignments, and part-time gigs that offer flexibility and the opportunity to leverage your skills and talents for extra income. Whether you're looking for a way to supplement your primary income or you desire a more flexible work arrangement, the gig economy provides various options for diversifying your income.

* **Freelance Work:** Freelancing encompasses a wide range of skills and industries, from writing and graphic design to web development and consulting. Platforms like Upwork, Freelancer, and Fiverr connect freelancers with clients seeking specific services. Freelancers have the flexibility to choose their projects, set their rates, and work on their terms.

* **Ridesharing and Delivery Services:** Companies like Uber, Lyft, and DoorDash have revolutionized the transportation and delivery industries. Becoming a rideshare or delivery driver offers a flexible way to earn income on your schedule. You can choose when and how often you want to work, making it a popular option for those looking to create additional income streams.

* **Online Marketplaces:** Online marketplaces such as Etsy, eBay, and Amazon allow individuals to sell products, crafts, vintage items, or used goods. Setting up an online store and marketing your products can be a rewarding way to generate income, especially if you have a passion for creating or curating unique items.

* **Remote Work:** With advancements in technology, remote work has become increasingly accessible. Many companies offer remote job opportunities across various fields, including customer service, marketing, and software development. Working remotely can provide a work-life balance and the flexibility to pursue other income-generating activities.

2. Side Hustles: Pursuing Part-Time Ventures

Side hustles are part-time businesses or ventures that you undertake alongside your primary job. They can range from selling products online to offering consulting services or running a small business. Side hustles offer the potential to supplement your income and, in some cases, even evolve into full-fledged businesses. Here are several side hustle ideas to consider:

177

* **E-commerce:** Launching an online store or selling products through platforms like Shopify or WooCommerce can be a lucrative side hustle. Whether you create your products or source them from suppliers, e-commerce allows you to reach a global audience and generate sales around the clock.

* **Consulting or Coaching:** If you possess expertise in a particular field, consider offering consulting or coaching services. Whether it's business consulting, career coaching, or personal finance advice, your knowledge and insights can help clients achieve their goals.

* **Freelance Writing:** If you have a way with words, freelance writing can be a rewarding side hustle. You can write articles, blog posts, or even e-books for clients in need of content. Freelance writing platforms like Contently and ProBlogger can connect you with potential clients.

* **Photography and Videography:** If you're passionate about photography or videography, you can offer your services for events, weddings, or corporate projects. Building a portfolio and marketing your work can lead to a steady stream of clients.

* **Pet Sitting or Dog Walking:** Animal lovers can explore pet-related side hustles, such as pet sitting or dog walking. Apps like Rover and Wag connect pet owners with caregivers, allowing you to earn income while spending time with furry companions.

3. Investment Income: Growing Your Wealth Passively

Investments are a powerful way to generate passive income over the long term. By putting your money to work in various assets, you can receive returns through dividends, interest payments, or capital appreciation. Here are common investment vehicles that can contribute to your income diversification:

* **Stocks:** Investing in stocks means owning a share of a company's ownership. Many publicly traded companies distribute dividends to their shareholders, providing a source of income. Additionally, stocks have the potential for capital appreciation, allowing you to sell shares at a higher price than your initial investment.

* **Real Estate:** Real estate investments can offer both rental income and potential property appreciation. You can invest in residential or commercial properties, or explore real estate investment trusts (REITs) for passive real estate income.

* **Bonds:** Bonds are debt securities issued by governments, municipalities, or corporations. When you invest in bonds, you receive periodic interest payments, typically semi-annually or annually. Bonds are known for their relatively lower risk compared to stocks.

* **Mutual Funds and ETFs:** Mutual funds and exchange-traded funds (ETFs) pool money from multiple investors to purchase a diversified portfolio of stocks, bonds, or other assets. They offer diversification and professional management. Mutual funds often distribute dividends and interest income to shareholders.

4. Rental Income: Owning and Leasing Properties

Rental income is a classic source of passive income that involves owning and leasing properties. Whether it's residential, commercial, or vacation rentals, real estate can provide a steady stream of rental income. Here are some key considerations for generating rental income:

* **Residential Rentals:** Residential properties, such as apartments, single-family homes, or duplexes, can generate rental

179

income from tenants. Becoming a landlord involves responsibilities like property maintenance, tenant management, and compliance with local regulations. To maximize rental income, it's essential to set competitive rental rates based on market trends, screen tenants carefully, and maintain the property's condition.

* **Commercial Rentals:** Commercial real estate, including office spaces, retail stores, and industrial properties, can offer higher rental income potential. Leasing to businesses often involves longer lease terms and lower tenant turnover. However, it may require a deeper understanding of commercial real estate markets.

* **Vacation Rentals:** Owning vacation properties in popular tourist destinations can provide seasonal rental income. Websites like Airbnb and Vrbo make it easier to market vacation rentals to travelers. Effective marketing, property maintenance, and guest satisfaction are crucial for success in this niche.

* **Real Estate Investment Trusts (REITs):** If direct property ownership isn't your preference, consider investing in real estate through REITs. REITs are companies that own or finance income-producing real estate in various sectors, such as residential, commercial, or healthcare. By investing in REITs, you can access diversified real estate portfolios and receive regular dividends.

5. Royalties and Intellectual Property: Earning from Creative Work

If you possess creative talents, intellectual property, or artistic abilities, you can earn royalties from your work. This income source can be particularly rewarding because it leverages your creative skills to generate passive income. Here are several avenues for earning royalties:

* **Books and Publications:** If you're an author or writer, you can earn royalties from book sales. Traditional publishing houses and self-publishing platforms like Amazon Kindle Direct Publishing offer opportunities to publish and sell your books globally.

* **Music and Recordings:** Musicians and composers receive royalties from the sale and streaming of their music. Licensing your compositions for use in films, commercials, or other media can also generate additional income.

* **Art and Visual Content:** Visual artists can earn royalties from the sale of their artwork, prints, or digital designs. Licensing your artwork for use in advertising, merchandise, or digital media can create ongoing revenue streams.

* **Patents and Inventions:** Inventors and innovators can earn royalties by licensing their patents or inventions to companies or individuals interested in using or manufacturing their technology. This approach is common in industries like technology and healthcare.

6. Online Ventures: Exploring Digital Opportunities

The internet has opened up various opportunities for income generation, making it possible to generate income online. These online ventures often require creativity, digital skills, and marketing savvy. Here are some online income options:

* **Affiliate Marketing:** Affiliate marketers promote products or services through affiliate programs and earn commissions for each sale or lead generated through their referral. Popular affiliate networks like Amazon Associates and ClickBank offer a wide range of products to promote.

* **E-commerce:** Starting an online store or selling products through platforms like Amazon or eBay allows you to reach a global audience. Dropshipping, where you sell products without holding inventory, is another e-commerce model to consider.

* **Blogging:** Blogging can be a profitable online venture if you create valuable content and attract a dedicated audience. Monetization methods include advertising, sponsored content, affiliate marketing, and selling digital products or courses.

* **Content Creation:** Platforms like YouTube and TikTok offer opportunities for content creators to monetize their videos through advertising revenue, sponsorships, merchandise sales, and fan support.

* **Online Courses and Digital Products:** If you have expertise in a particular field, you can create and sell online courses, e-books, templates, or digital products. Marketplaces like Udemy and Teachable provide platforms for course creation and sales.

* **Freelance Work:** The gig economy isn't limited to physical locations; many freelance opportunities are available online. You can offer services like writing, graphic design, web development, or digital marketing to clients worldwide.

These online ventures offer the advantage of accessibility and scalability, allowing you to reach a global audience and potentially generate income around the clock. However, success often requires dedication, consistent effort, and a solid online presence.

Success Stories in Income Diversification

To illustrate the transformative potential of income diversification, let's delve into real-life case studies of individuals who successfully built multiple income streams:

Case Study 1: The Freelance Entrepreneur

Emily's Journey to Financial Freedom

Emily, a marketing professional with years of experience, found herself increasingly dissatisfied with the monotony of her full-time job. She yearned for more creative freedom and control over her work. The gig economy was rapidly expanding, and Emily saw an opportunity to turn her passion and skills into a lucrative freelance business.

The Early Days: Navigating Freelancing

In the beginning, Emily decided to take her first tentative steps into the world of freelancing. She kept her full-time job and began offering marketing services in her spare time. Her first clients were acquaintances who needed help with small projects. This allowed her to build her portfolio and gain experience in working directly with clients.

Balancing Act: Part-Time Freelancing

Balancing her full-time job and freelance work was initially challenging for Emily. Late nights and weekends were dedicated to client projects and building her online presence. She invested time in creating a professional website, showcasing her skills, and networking on social media platforms.

As her client base slowly grew, Emily began to see the potential of freelancing as a source of additional income. The extra money she earned was initially saved and invested, gradually helping her build a financial buffer.

Transition to Full-Time Freelancing

Emily's journey to full-time freelancing was marked by a series of key milestones. She knew that quitting her secure job to pursue freelancing full-time was a significant step, and she wanted to ensure her financial security.

First, she consistently built her client base, which included local businesses, startups, and even some international clients. Emily's reputation as a reliable and creative marketing professional continued to grow, leading to word-of-mouth referrals.

Second, she paid off her outstanding debts, including her student loans and car loan. Emily understood that reducing financial obligations would provide her with more flexibility and less financial pressure when transitioning to full-time freelancing.

Third, Emily built a financial safety net. She created an emergency fund equivalent to six months of living expenses, ensuring that she could cover her basic needs and business expenses even during lean months.

Achieving Financial Freedom

When Emily finally made the leap to full-time freelancing, she was well-prepared both financially and professionally. Her commitment to delivering high-quality work and her growing network of satisfied clients allowed her to thrive in the competitive freelance market.

As her income from freelancing steadily increased, Emily focused on maintaining a sustainable work-life balance. She set boundaries on her working hours, took regular breaks, and prioritized self-care. This approach not only ensured her well-being but also enhanced her productivity and creativity.

Emily's freelance business continued to flourish. She diversified her income by offering various marketing services, including content creation, social media management, and digital advertising. This allowed her to weather fluctuations in demand for specific services and maintain a stable income.

Today, Emily enjoys both financial security and the flexibility to work on projects she's passionate about. She attributes her success to her determination, commitment to quality, and strategic financial planning. Emily's journey serves as a testament to the opportunities available in the gig economy and the potential for individuals to achieve financial independence while doing what they love.

Case Study 2: The Real Estate Investor

David's Path to Wealth Through Real Estate

David, a software engineer with a stable job and a passion for investing, had always been fascinated by real estate. He recognized the potential of real estate as a means to diversify his income and build long-term wealth. David's journey into real estate investing would eventually become a significant part of his financial success.

Initial Investments: Navigating the Real Estate Market

David started his real estate journey by purchasing his first rental property in his early thirties. He conducted extensive research on the local real estate market, seeking areas with high demand and strong potential for property appreciation. After careful consideration, he settled on a modest residential property in a growing neighborhood.

He financed the purchase with a combination of his savings and a mortgage. David understood that leveraging debt could amplify his investment returns if managed wisely.

Property management was an essential aspect of David's real estate strategy. He chose to manage his properties himself initially, learning about tenant management, maintenance, and property accounting along the way. This hands-on approach allowed him to maximize rental income and minimize expenses.

Expanding the Portfolio: Growing Rental Income

As David's career in software engineering progressed, so did his real estate investments. He continued to acquire additional residential properties, each carefully selected based on location, potential rental income, and long-term appreciation prospects.

David's real estate portfolio gradually became a substantial source of passive income. Rental income from his properties provided financial stability and served as a significant complement to his primary job income. He reinvested a portion of the rental income into property improvements and maintenance, ensuring the long-term value of his investments.

Transitioning to Full-Time Investor

Over the years, David's real estate investments evolved into a substantial portfolio. He began to see the potential of transitioning to full-time real estate investing. However, he knew that such a transition required careful planning and financial security.

First, David continued to educate himself about real estate investing. He attended seminars, networked with experienced investors, and sought advice from mentors. This continuous learning allowed him to refine his investment strategies and identify new opportunities.

Second, he built a financial safety net. David established an emergency fund, ensuring that he had sufficient cash reserves to cover unexpected property expenses and income gaps during tenant turnovers.

Third, David gradually reduced his reliance on his software engineering job. He diversified his income by exploring additional real estate investment avenues, such as commercial properties and real estate investment trusts (REITs). These ventures generated passive income, further strengthening his financial position.

When David eventually made the transition to full-time real estate investing, he was well-prepared. His diversified real estate portfolio provided him with a consistent stream of rental income, and the additional income streams he had developed over the years contributed to his financial security.

Financial Independence and Legacy

Today, David enjoys financial independence through his successful real estate ventures. His income from rental properties, commercial investments, and REITs allows him to have greater control over his time and life choices. David's journey from a software engineer to a full-time real estate investor demonstrates the potential for individuals to achieve financial independence by strategically building income streams outside of traditional employment.

Case Study 3: The Creative Entrepreneur

Sara's Pursuit of Artistic Passion and Financial Independence

Sara, an artist and writer with a deep love for creativity, found herself in a corporate job that left her unfulfilled. While the job provided financial security, it did not align with her passion for art and writing. Sara knew she needed a change and decided to explore opportunities that would allow her to pursue her creative interests while still securing her financial future.

The Turning Point: Embracing Creative Ventures

Sara began her journey by starting a blog dedicated to her love for art and writing. She shared her thoughts, stories, and artwork with the world, gradually building an online presence and a loyal readership. While the blog didn't generate significant income initially, it became a platform for Sara to showcase her creative talents.

Simultaneously, Sara began publishing e-books and selling her artwork online. She realized that her passion could be transformed into income-generating ventures. These endeavors allowed her to monetize her creativity, albeit on a small scale at first.

The Growth Phase: Expanding Online Presence

As Sara's online presence continued to grow, so did her income. She leveraged affiliate marketing by promoting products and services related to her niche, earning commissions for referrals. Sara's blog became a hub for art enthusiasts and writers alike, generating advertising revenue and sponsorships.

She expanded her e-book offerings, catering to a niche audience interested in her unique style of storytelling and art. These digital products provided a steady stream of passive income.

Sara's commitment to her creative ventures was unwavering. She continued to create and share content that resonated with her audience, fostering a sense of community and engagement.

Financial Independence and Creative Freedom

Over time, Sara's diversified income streams began to provide substantial financial stability. While her corporate job remained her primary income source, her creative ventures were steadily growing.

As her online income increased, Sara made strategic financial decisions. She paid off her outstanding debts, including student loans and credit card balances. This reduced her financial obligations and allowed her to allocate more resources to her creative projects.

With a financial safety net in place, Sara took a significant leap. She decided to transition from her corporate job to pursue her artistic passions full-time. This decision was driven by her desire for creative freedom and her growing confidence in her ability to generate income through her art and writing.

Sara's transition to full-time creative entrepreneurship was marked by a renewed sense of purpose and fulfillment. She dedicated her time to producing high-quality content, expanding her e-book offerings, and collaborating with fellow artists and writers.

Today, Sara enjoys financial independence while pursuing her artistic passions full-time. Her income from her blog, e-books, affiliate marketing, and artwork sales provides her with both financial security and the creative freedom she longed for.

Sara's journey serves as a powerful example of how individuals can align their passion with income generation, ultimately achieving financial independence while doing what they love. It underscores the importance of pursuing one's creative interests and strategically building diversified income streams to secure both financial and personal fulfillment.

Strategies for Building Multiple Income Streams

Now that we've explored the concept of income diversification and learned from real-life success stories, let's delve into strategies for creating and nurturing multiple income streams:

Unlocking Additional Income Streams: Strategies for Financial Growth

In an ever-evolving economic landscape, the pursuit of financial growth and stability often leads individuals to explore opportunities beyond their primary income source. Whether driven by the desire to achieve financial independence, increase savings, or pursue personal passions, the quest for additional income streams has become a crucial aspect of modern financial planning.

This chapter delves into the strategies and practical steps that individuals can take to identify, create, and manage multiple income streams effectively. By leveraging skills, interests, and resources, you can unlock the potential for financial growth and enhance your financial well-being.

1. Identify Your Skills and Interests: Unleashing Your Earning Potential

The journey to diversifying income streams begins with self-assessment. Identifying your unique skills, passions, and areas of expertise forms the foundation for creating additional income opportunities. By recognizing your strengths, you can leverage them to generate income in various ways. Here's how you can begin:

* Self-Reflection: Take time to reflect on your skills, experiences, and interests. Consider the activities or tasks that come naturally

to you, as well as those you are passionate about. Identify your strengths, both in your professional and personal life.

* Marketable Skills: Assess the marketability of your skills. Are there specific skills or knowledge areas that are in demand in your industry or niche? Keep in mind that skills that are valuable to others can often be monetized.

* Identify Gaps: Identify gaps in the market or opportunities where your skills and interests intersect. This is where you can offer unique value and potentially create income streams.

2. Explore the Gig Economy: Freelancing and Consulting

The gig economy has emerged as a significant driver of income diversification, offering flexible work arrangements and opportunities for skilled professionals to connect with clients. Platforms like Upwork, Freelancer, and Fiverr have created a marketplace for freelancers and consultants to offer their expertise. Here's how you can leverage the gig economy:

* Skill Utilization: Assess your skills and consider if they can be applied to freelancing or consulting work. Common fields include graphic design, writing, web development, marketing, and consulting in various industries.

* Online Presence: Establish an online presence through a professional profile on freelancing platforms. Highlight your skills, experience, and past projects. An impressive portfolio and client reviews can boost your credibility.

* Networking: Build a network of potential clients by actively bidding on relevant projects and networking within your industry. Attend webinars, forums, and conferences to connect with potential clients.

191

* Time Management: Efficiently manage your time between your primary job and freelance work. Create a schedule that allows you to deliver quality work to clients without compromising your full-time commitments.

* Deliver Value: Consistently deliver high-quality work to clients. Your reputation as a reliable and skilled freelancer can lead to repeat business and referrals.

3. Start a Side Hustle: Passion Projects with Profit Potential

A side hustle refers to a part-time business or venture that individuals pursue alongside their primary job. It's an opportunity to turn hobbies, interests, or expertise into income-generating activities. Here's how to get started:

* Identify Your Passion: Consider your hobbies, interests, or areas where you have expertise. A successful side hustle is often built on something you are passionate about.

* Market Research: Conduct market research to assess the demand for your chosen side hustle. Are there potential customers or clients who would be interested in your products or services?

* Business Plan: Develop a business plan outlining your side hustle's goals, target audience, pricing strategy, and marketing plan. A clear plan provides direction and increases your chances of success.

* Time Management: Efficiently allocate your time between your primary job, side hustle, and personal life. Create a schedule that allows you to work on your side hustle without overwhelming yourself.

192

* Scale Gradually: Start small and scale your side hustle gradually as it gains momentum. Reinvest profits into growing your business and expanding your offerings.

4. Invest for Passive Income: Building Wealth Through Investments

Investing is a powerful way to create passive income streams. By allocating capital to assets that generate returns, such as dividends, interest, or rental income, you can build wealth over time. Here are steps to consider when pursuing passive income through investments:

* Investment Portfolio: Diversify your investment portfolio across different asset classes, such as stocks, bonds, real estate, and mutual funds. Diversification helps spread risk and potentially enhance returns.

* Research and Due Diligence: Conduct thorough research before making investment decisions. Understand the assets you're investing in, the risks associated with them, and their potential for generating passive income.

* Risk Tolerance: Assess your risk tolerance and align your investments accordingly. Your risk tolerance depends on factors such as your age, financial goals, and comfort with market volatility.

* Asset Allocation: Develop an asset allocation strategy that suits your financial objectives. Determine the percentage of your portfolio allocated to income-generating assets versus growth-oriented assets.

* Passive Income Streams: Identify investments that are known for generating passive income. These may include dividend-

paying stocks, bonds with interest payments, or real estate
properties that produce rental income.

* Diversify for Stability: Consider diversifying your passive
income sources to reduce risk. This might involve spreading your
investments across different stocks, bonds, or properties.

* Professional Advice: Seek advice from financial advisors or
professionals, especially for complex investments or retirement
planning. Expert guidance can help you make informed
investment decisions.

**5. Create Online Income Streams: Leveraging the Digital
World * Leveraging the Digital World: The internet has opened
up numerous opportunities to create online income streams.
Whether through content creation, e-commerce, or affiliate
marketing, the digital realm offers a vast landscape for income
generation. Here's how to make the most of it:

Content Creation: Start a blog, YouTube channel, or podcast
dedicated to a niche you are passionate about. Consistently
produce high-quality content that appeals to your target audience.
As your online presence grows, you can monetize your content
through advertising, sponsorships, and affiliate marketing.

E-commerce Ventures: Consider launching an e-commerce
store to sell products or digital goods. Platforms like Shopify,
WooCommerce, and Etsy make it relatively easy to set up online
shops. Research your target market, source products, and
establish a marketing strategy to drive sales.

Affiliate Marketing: Affiliate marketing involves promoting
products or services on your platform and earning a commission
for each sale or lead generated through your referral. Partner with
affiliate programs relevant to your niche and create valuable
content that encourages conversions.

Social Media Influence: If you have a significant following on social media platforms like Instagram or TikTok, you can collaborate with brands for sponsored posts and promotional campaigns. Social media influence can be monetized through brand partnerships and endorsements.

Online Courses and Webinars: Share your expertise by offering online courses or webinars. Create educational content on subjects you're knowledgeable about and use platforms like Udemy, Teachable, or Zoom to deliver courses. Earnings come from course fees or ticket sales.

Monetizing Apps and Software: If you have coding or development skills, consider creating mobile apps or software solutions. You can generate income through app sales, in-app purchases, or subscriptions.

6. Network and Collaborate: Expanding Opportunities

Networking and collaboration can lead to new income opportunities and business ventures. Building relationships within your industry or niche opens doors to partnerships, joint ventures, and referrals. Here's how to harness the power of networking:

* Attend Industry Events: Participate in conferences, workshops, and industry-specific events to connect with professionals in your field. These gatherings provide opportunities to exchange ideas and explore potential collaborations.

* Join Professional Groups: Become a member of professional organizations, online forums, or LinkedIn groups related to your industry. Engaging in discussions, sharing insights, and offering help can lead to valuable connections.

* Collaborate with Peers: Identify potential collaborators or individuals with complementary skills. Collaborative projects, whether they involve co-authoring a book, developing a product, or launching a joint venture, can create new income streams.

* Networking Platforms: Utilize networking platforms like LinkedIn to connect with professionals in your industry or niche. Customize your LinkedIn profile to highlight your skills and expertise.

* Offer Referral Incentives: Encourage referrals by offering incentives to your network. Whether it's a referral fee, a discount on your services, or another mutually beneficial arrangement, referrals can lead to new clients and income.

7. Time Management: Maximizing Productivity and Balance

Efficiently managing your time is crucial when pursuing multiple income streams. Balancing your primary job, side ventures, and personal life requires effective time management. Here's how to optimize your time:

* Prioritize Tasks: Identify your most important tasks and allocate time to them. Use techniques like the Eisenhower Matrix to categorize tasks as urgent and important, non-urgent but important, urgent but not important, or neither.

* Create a Schedule: Develop a schedule that includes dedicated blocks of time for your primary job, side hustles, and personal life. Stick to your schedule to maintain balance and productivity.

* Set Clear Goals: Define clear and achievable goals for each of your income streams. Having specific objectives helps you stay focused and measure your progress.

* Avoid Overcommitment: Be cautious not to overextend yourself. Ensure that your commitments align with your available time and energy.

* Delegate and Automate: Consider delegating tasks or automating processes whenever possible. This can help streamline your workflow and free up time for high-priority activities.

* Regularly Review and Adjust: Periodically review your time management strategies and adjust them as needed. Reflect on what's working well and where improvements can be made.

Your Path to Income Diversification**

The pursuit of multiple income streams is a dynamic journey that can lead to financial growth, security, and personal fulfillment. By identifying your skills, exploring opportunities in the gig economy, starting side hustles, investing wisely, creating online income streams, networking, and efficiently managing your time, you can unlock the potential for financial success.

Each individual's path to income diversification is unique, shaped by personal interests, goals, and circumstances. Whether you're looking to increase savings, achieve financial independence, or simply pursue your passions, the strategies outlined in this chapter provide a roadmap for unleashing your earning potential.

As you embark on this journey, remember that success often requires dedication, resilience, and adaptability. Stay committed to your goals, continuously seek opportunities for growth, and embrace the entrepreneurial spirit within you. The quest for multiple income streams is not only about financial gain but also about expanding your horizons, exploring your passions, and creating a life of greater possibilities.

Empowering Your Financial Future**

197

Building multiple income streams is a dynamic strategy that empowers your financial future. It diversifies your income sources, enhances financial security, and accelerates wealth accumulation. As you explore the gig economy, side hustles, investments, and other avenues for additional income, remember that income diversification is not a one-size-fits-all approach. It's a personalized strategy that aligns with your skills, interests, and financial goals.

In the chapters that follow, we will delve into advanced wealth-building strategies and financial concepts, equipping you with the knowledge and tools to continue your journey to wealth mastery.

Chapter 8: Legacy and Philanthropy

As we journey towards wealth mastery, we encounter a profound and transformative stage: the exploration of legacy and philanthropy. Beyond the accumulation of wealth, the impact we leave on the world and the joy of giving back become defining elements of our financial journey. In this chapter, we will discuss the significance of leaving a financial legacy, explore philanthropic opportunities, and delve into the deeply rewarding act of giving back. We will also showcase stories of individuals who have made a meaningful impact through their wealth, demonstrating the extraordinary potential of legacy and philanthropy.

The Essence of Leaving a Legacy

Leaving a legacy goes beyond passing on material possessions; it involves passing on values, wisdom, and a lasting impact. It's about making a positive contribution to the lives of future generations and society at large. Let's explore the importance of leaving a financial legacy:

1. Perpetuating Values: The Essence of Legacy

A financial legacy is not just about leaving behind assets; it's about passing on your principles, values, and life lessons to future generations. It ensures that the wisdom you've acquired throughout your journey continues to shape and inspire those who come after you.

a. Values-Driven Wealth: One of the core elements of a meaningful legacy is the alignment of your wealth with your values. What do you hold dear in life? What principles guide your actions? Your financial legacy should reflect these values. For instance, if you value education, your legacy might include funding scholarships or endowing educational institutions.

199

b. Teaching by Example: Your actions and decisions throughout your life are a testament to your values. By demonstrating responsible financial stewardship and philanthropy, you set an example for your heirs to follow. Your legacy can be a living testament to the importance of ethical and thoughtful financial management.

c. Family Values: Within your family, a financial legacy can serve as a bridge between generations. It can encapsulate the collective wisdom, cultural heritage, and shared values of your family. Passing on these values fosters a sense of continuity and unity.

2. Supporting Loved Ones: Ensuring Their Prosperity

One of the most impactful ways to leave a financial legacy is by providing support and security to your loved ones. It allows you to empower them to pursue their dreams, ambitions, and life goals without the burden of financial constraints.

a. Family Financial Security: A well-planned legacy can offer financial stability and protection to your family. It ensures that your spouse, children, and future generations have a safety net to fall back on in times of need.

b. Educational Opportunities: Supporting the educational pursuits of your descendants is a powerful way to leave a lasting impact. Establishing education funds or scholarships can open doors for younger family members and enable them to achieve their academic goals.

c. Entrepreneurial Ventures: If entrepreneurship runs in your family, consider fostering a culture of innovation and enterprise by providing seed capital or resources for business ventures. Your legacy can fuel the entrepreneurial spirit for generations to come.

3. Impacting Causes You Care About: The Power of Philanthropy

A significant component of a meaningful financial legacy is philanthropy. It allows you to contribute to causes and organizations that resonate with your values and passions. Your legacy can be a force for positive change in the world.

a. Cause-Aligned Giving: Identify the causes that matter most to you. Whether it's environmental conservation, healthcare, education, or poverty alleviation, your legacy can be a driving force for positive change in these areas.

b. Establishing Foundations: Consider establishing a charitable foundation or trust that will carry out your philanthropic objectives. Foundations can continue your philanthropic work for generations, supporting various charitable endeavors.

c. Collaborative Giving: Encourage your family members to participate in your philanthropic endeavors. Involving your heirs in charitable giving fosters a sense of responsibility and shared values.

4. Leaving a Mark on Society: A Legacy Beyond Borders

Your financial legacy can extend far beyond your immediate family, reaching out to touch and uplift society at large. It has the potential to fund research, support education, address pressing social issues, and contribute to the betterment of humanity.

a. Supporting Research and Innovation: Scientific research and innovation often require substantial funding. Your legacy can sponsor research initiatives that have the potential to solve critical global challenges, from healthcare breakthroughs to renewable energy solutions.

b. Educational Endowments: Endowing educational institutions, scholarships, and research centers can transform lives and communities. It ensures that knowledge and learning thrive for generations.

c. Addressing Social Challenges: Many pressing social issues, such as poverty, inequality, and environmental degradation, require concerted efforts and resources. Your legacy can fund organizations and initiatives dedicated to addressing these challenges.

Crafting Your Legacy: Practical Steps

Creating a meaningful financial legacy requires careful planning and consideration. Here are practical steps to help you design and execute your legacy plan:

1. Clarify Your Values: Begin by identifying your core values and principles. Reflect on what truly matters to you, both personally and socially. Your values will serve as the foundation of your legacy.

2. Set Clear Objectives: Define your legacy objectives. What impact do you want to have on your family, community, or the world? Setting specific goals will guide your planning.

3. Seek Professional Guidance: Consider consulting with financial advisors, estate planners, and philanthropy experts to help you navigate the complexities of legacy planning. They can assist in structuring your assets and establishing mechanisms for your legacy.

4. Create a Will and Estate Plan: Draft a comprehensive will and estate plan that outlines how your assets will be distributed and used to fulfill your legacy objectives. Ensure that your wishes are legally documented.

5. Establish Trusts and Foundations: If your legacy involves significant philanthropic or educational endeavors, consider setting up trusts or foundations. These entities can carry out your objectives and provide continuity beyond your lifetime.

6. Involve Family Members: If family values and unity are integral to your legacy, involve your family members in the planning process. Encourage open discussions about your legacy goals and values.

7. Continually Review and Adjust: As circumstances change, revisit your legacy plan periodically to ensure it remains aligned with your values and objectives. Update your plan as needed to accommodate evolving priorities.

Creating a meaningful financial legacy is a profound expression of your values, beliefs, and aspirations. It transcends the accumulation of wealth and becomes a vehicle for positive change and enduring influence. Your legacy can touch the lives of your loved ones, support causes close to your heart, and leave an indelible mark on society.

Exploring Philanthropic Opportunities

Philanthropy is the act of giving back to the community or society through financial contributions, time, or expertise. It is a powerful way to create a positive impact and find profound fulfillment. Here are some philanthropic opportunities to consider:

1. Charitable Giving: A Heartfelt Commitment

"The smallest act of kindness is worth more than the grandest intention." — Oscar Wilde

Charitable giving forms the bedrock of philanthropy. It embodies the spirit of compassion and empathy, transforming your financial resources into a force for good. Whether you choose to support local charities, global causes, or a blend of both, your donations can significantly impact the lives of those in need.

A. The Power of Intention: Charitable giving begins with intention. It's a conscious choice to allocate a portion of your resources to support causes aligned with your values and beliefs. When done thoughtfully and sincerely, it becomes a powerful tool for creating a legacy of compassion and generosity.

B. Aligning with Your Values: To maximize the impact of your charitable giving, consider your core values and areas of personal significance. Are you passionate about education, healthcare, environmental conservation, poverty alleviation, or arts and culture? Identifying your areas of focus will guide your philanthropic journey.

C. Research and Due Diligence: Not all charitable organizations are created equal. As you embark on your giving journey, invest time in researching and selecting reputable charities. Look for organizations with a track record of transparent financial management and a history of effectively channeling donations toward their missions.

D. Consistency Matters: The impact of charitable giving often grows over time. Regular, consistent donations can provide sustained support to organizations and causes. Consider creating a giving plan that outlines your annual or monthly charitable contributions.

E. Beyond Financial Resources: While monetary donations are vital, don't underestimate the value of non-financial contributions. Your time, skills, and knowledge can be equally impactful. Volunteering for a cause you care about or offering your expertise to a nonprofit organization amplifies your philanthropic efforts.

F. Tax Advantages: In many countries, charitable contributions come with tax benefits. Be sure to understand the tax implications of your giving and take advantage of any available deductions or credits.

G. Legacy of Compassion: Charitable giving isn't just about the present; it's about the future. By making philanthropy a part of your financial legacy, you leave behind a legacy of compassion, generosity, and social responsibility.

2. Establishing a Foundation: A Dedicated Commitment

"The foundation stones for a balanced success are honesty, character, integrity, faith, love, and loyalty." — Zig Ziglar

For those who possess the means and a profound dedication to a specific cause, establishing a charitable foundation can be a transformative step in creating a lasting legacy. A foundation allows you to have a direct, sustained impact on the causes and initiatives you hold dear.

A. Vision and Mission: The establishment of a charitable foundation begins with a clear vision and mission. What are the objectives of your foundation? What issues or areas will it address? Your vision should resonate with your values and serve as a guiding light for your philanthropic efforts.

B. Legal Structure: Foundations come in various legal structures, including private foundations, family foundations, and public foundations. Each has its own regulatory requirements and tax implications. Consulting with legal and financial advisors is essential in determining the most suitable structure for your foundation.

C. Funding the Foundation: One of the critical decisions is how to fund your foundation. This can involve a significant financial commitment, often through a one-time endowment or regular contributions. Your foundation's financial sustainability is paramount to its ability to effect change over time.

D. Governance and Administration: Foundations require governance structures that ensure transparency, accountability, and responsible management of funds. Boards of directors, trustees, and administrators play key roles in guiding the foundation's activities.

E. Grant-Making Strategy: Your foundation's impact is realized through grant-making. Develop a clear strategy for identifying, vetting, and supporting charitable organizations or projects. Your strategy should align with your foundation's mission and goals.

F. Measuring Impact: Effective foundations embrace a culture of impact measurement and evaluation. Establish metrics and key performance indicators (KPIs) to assess the outcomes and effectiveness of your philanthropic initiatives.

G. Collaboration and Partnerships: Foundations can amplify their impact by collaborating with other philanthropic entities, nonprofits, government agencies, and businesses. Partnerships can leverage resources and expertise to address complex challenges.

H. Legacy Planning: Consider the long-term sustainability of your foundation. Outline succession plans, governance transitions, and funding mechanisms to ensure that your foundation continues to fulfill its mission for generations to come.

I. Family and Succession: If your foundation is a family foundation, involve family members in its governance and decision-making. Educate future generations about the foundation's mission and values, ensuring a seamless transition of leadership.

J. Fulfilling a Passion: A foundation provides a platform to channel your passion and resources into meaningful action. It allows you to make a tangible difference in areas that resonate deeply with you.

3. Volunteerism: The Gift of Time and Expertise

**"Volunteering is the art of giving, leading, and inspiring." — Anurag Prakash Ray

Beyond financial contributions, the gift of time and expertise through volunteerism can be a potent means of creating a lasting impact. Your skills and knowledge can bring transformative change to nonprofit organizations, community projects, and initiatives you are passionate about.

A. The Heart of Volunteerism: Volunteering is rooted in the desire to make a positive difference. It involves dedicating your time, energy, and skills toward causes or organizations that rely on the support of individuals like you. Volunteering is a manifestation of empathy and a tangible expression of your commitment to creating a better world.

B. Identifying Opportunities: To get started with volunteerism, begin by identifying opportunities that align with your skills, interests, and values. Local nonprofits, community organizations, schools, and religious institutions often seek volunteers for a range of initiatives.

C. Skills-Based Volunteering: Consider the unique skills and expertise you possess. Skills-based volunteering allows you to leverage your professional or personal talents to address specific needs within organizations. For instance, if you have marketing skills, you could assist a nonprofit in crafting effective communication strategies.

D. Nonprofit and NGO Engagement: Many nonprofits and non-governmental organizations (NGOs) rely on volunteers to carry out their missions. These organizations tackle a wide array of issues, from hunger and homelessness to education and environmental conservation. Explore causes that resonate with you, and inquire about volunteer opportunities.

E. Community Involvement: Local communities often benefit significantly from volunteer support. You can engage in community-building initiatives, such as neighborhood cleanups, youth mentorship programs, or senior citizen outreach. Building a strong sense of community fosters a positive environment for everyone.

F. Remote and Virtual Volunteering: In today's interconnected world, volunteering isn't limited by geographical boundaries. Many organizations offer remote or virtual volunteer opportunities, allowing you to contribute your skills and time from anywhere.

G. Corporate Volunteering: Some employers encourage and facilitate employee volunteering by offering paid time off for volunteer activities. Corporate volunteering programs can provide a structured and supportive environment for your philanthropic endeavors.

H. Impact Measurement: Like financial philanthropy, volunteerism benefits from impact measurement and evaluation. Understanding the outcomes and effectiveness of your volunteer efforts helps you refine your contributions and make a more significant impact.

I. Mentoring and Education: Sharing your knowledge and expertise through mentoring or educational programs can be a profound form of volunteerism. You empower individuals with the tools and guidance they need to thrive and succeed.

J. A Ripple Effect: The impact of volunteerism often extends far beyond the immediate beneficiaries. It can inspire others to join in, creating a ripple effect of positive change within communities and organizations.

K. Time as a Precious Gift: In a world where time is often scarce, dedicating your time to support causes you care about is a precious gift. Your commitment to volunteerism can be an enduring part of your legacy, demonstrating your values and commitment to making a difference.

4. Impact Investing: Aligning Profits with Purpose

"Investing is not about making money. It's about making dreams come true." — Naveen Jain

Impact investing represents a dynamic intersection of finance and philanthropy. It involves making investments with the dual intention of generating financial returns and effecting positive social or environmental impacts. Impact investors seek to align their capital with their values, using their financial resources as a force for good.

A. Investment with Purpose: Impact investing is a conscious choice to allocate capital toward businesses, organizations, or projects that address pressing social or environmental challenges. These investments can span various sectors, from renewable energy and affordable housing to education and healthcare.

B. Measurement and Metrics: Impact investors emphasize the measurement and evaluation of their investments' social and environmental outcomes. They use metrics such as social return on investment (SROI) and environmental impact assessments to assess the effectiveness of their investments.

C. Diverse Investment Vehicles: Impact investments can take various forms, including equity investments, debt instruments, private equity, venture capital, and more. Impact investors diversify their portfolios across these vehicles to spread risk while maximizing impact.

D. Addressing Global Challenges: Impact investing directly addresses global challenges such as climate change, poverty alleviation, access to clean water, and gender equality. It provides a financial solution to some of the world's most pressing issues.

E. Blended Finance: In some cases, impact investors collaborate with governments, philanthropic organizations, and development agencies in a concept known as blended finance. This approach combines public and private resources to scale impact-focused projects and initiatives.

F. Positive Screening: Impact investors often employ positive screening criteria when selecting investments. They proactively seek opportunities that align with their values and impact goals, actively seeking out ventures making a difference.

G. Financial Returns: While impact investors prioritize social and environmental impact, they do not ignore financial returns. They expect their investments to generate competitive returns, creating a sustainable cycle of capital allocation.

H. Direct and Indirect Impact: Impact investments can create both direct and indirect impact. Direct impact occurs when investments directly contribute to a social or environmental outcome, such as financing a clean energy project. Indirect impact may result from investments in companies that adopt sustainable practices and influence industry standards.

I. Portfolio Diversification: Impact investors recognize the importance of diversifying their impact portfolios. By spreading investments across different sectors and asset classes, they mitigate risks while expanding their reach.

J. Empowering Entrepreneurs: Impact investing empowers entrepreneurs and innovators to develop solutions to pressing challenges. It provides the financial resources needed to bring impactful ideas to fruition.

K. Global Philanthropic Networks: Impact investors often connect with global philanthropic networks and impact-oriented organizations to identify opportunities and collaborate on initiatives that align with their values.

L. Shaping a Better Future: Impact investing embodies the belief that financial resources can play a pivotal role in shaping a better future. It enables individuals to play an active role in addressing global issues and advancing solutions to the world's most pressing challenges.

5. Scholarship Programs: Empowering Future Generations

"Education is the most powerful weapon you can use to change the world." — Nelson Mandela

Scholarship programs offer a powerful means of supporting education and empowering individuals to achieve their academic and career goals. By establishing or contributing to scholarship initiatives, you can leave a legacy that fosters learning, growth, and opportunity.

A. The Transformative Power of Education: Scholarships recognize the transformative potential of education. They provide access to learning opportunities that can reshape lives, open doors, and unlock new possibilities.

B. Tailoring Your Focus: Scholarship programs allow you to tailor your support to specific areas or fields of study that align with your valucs and interests. Whether you prioritize STEM (science, technology, engineering, and mathematics), the arts, or social sciences, your scholarships can create a lasting impact.

C. Enabling Access: Many individuals face financial barriers to pursuing higher education. Scholarships remove these obstacles by covering tuition, fees, books, and living expenses. This enables students to concentrate on their studies rather than financial worries.

D. Academic Excellence: Scholarships often reward academic excellence, providing recognition and motivation for outstanding students to continue excelling in their studies.

E. Need-Based Scholarships: Beyond academic achievement, need-based scholarships address financial need. These scholarships ensure that students with limited financial resources have equal opportunities to pursue education.

F. Supporting Underrepresented Groups: Scholarship programs can prioritize underrepresented or marginalized groups, including minority students, women in STEM fields, or individuals with disabilities. By doing so, you contribute to diversity, equity, and inclusion in education.

G. Geographic Reach: Scholarship programs can extend beyond national borders. They can support students locally, nationally, or globally, broadening your impact and reach.

H. Beyond Financial Support: Scholarships often include mentorship and support programs that guide recipients throughout their academic journeys. This holistic approach increases the chances of academic success and future contributions to society.

I. Legacy of Learning: Scholarships reflect your commitment to education and the belief that knowledge is a powerful force for positive change. They leave a legacy of enlightenment, growth, and empowerment for future generations.

J. Selection and Criteria: When establishing a scholarship program, consider the selection criteria carefully. Determine the eligibility requirements, application process, and evaluation criteria to ensure that your scholarships align with your goals and values.

K. Endowing Scholarships: To create a lasting impact, you can choose to endow scholarships, which means investing a significant sum of money to establish a perpetual scholarship fund. Endowed scholarships continue to support students indefinitely, even beyond your lifetime.

L. Alumni Engagement: Engaging with scholarship recipients can foster a sense of community and connection. Many scholarship donors develop relationships with students, which can lead to ongoing support and mentorship.

M. Partnering with Educational Institutions: Collaborating with educational institutions, such as colleges, universities, or trade schools, can streamline the administration of scholarship programs. Educational institutions often have expertise in managing scholarships and selecting recipients.

N. Celebrating Achievements: Recognize and celebrate the achievements of scholarship recipients. By doing so, you highlight the impact of your scholarships and inspire others to support education.

O. The Gift of Knowledge: Scholarships are, in essence, the gift of knowledge and opportunity. They empower individuals to become future leaders, innovators, and contributors to society.

The Joy of Giving Back

Philanthropy is not just about financial contributions; it's also about the joy of giving back to others and making a difference. Giving back can bring profound fulfillment and a sense of purpose. Here's why giving back is so rewarding:

1. Fulfillment: The Joy of Giving

At the core of philanthropy lies the joy of giving—embracing the opportunity to make a positive difference in the lives of others and contribute to the greater good. It's a sentiment deeply rooted in the human experience, one that transcends wealth and status. Here, we explore how philanthropy brings a profound sense of fulfillment to both donors and recipients.

A. The Power of Empathy

Philanthropy often begins with empathy—a capacity to understand and share the feelings of others. When you empathize with those facing challenges or injustice, it stirs a desire to take action, to alleviate suffering, and to uplift individuals and

214

communities. This innate sense of compassion sparks the journey of philanthropy.

B. A Deeper Sense of Purpose

Engaging in philanthropy provides a profound sense of purpose. It amplifies the meaning of wealth and success, shifting the focus from accumulation to contribution. It aligns your actions with your values, reflecting a commitment to leaving the world better than you found it. This alignment nurtures a sense of fulfillment that transcends material wealth.

C. The Joy of Impact

Witnessing the impact of your philanthropic efforts generates immeasurable joy. Whether it's seeing a child's smile after receiving an education scholarship or witnessing a community flourish due to clean water initiatives, the tangible outcomes of your generosity bring a deep and lasting sense of fulfillment.

D. A Reflection of Abundance

Philanthropy arises from a belief in abundance—an understanding that you have the capacity to share and enrich the lives of others. By practicing philanthropy, you shift from a mindset of scarcity to one of plenty, recognizing that your resources can create positive change.

E. Emotional Well-Being

Studies have consistently shown that acts of philanthropy are associated with increased emotional well-being. Giving elicits feelings of happiness, gratitude, and connectedness, reducing stress and enhancing overall mental health. It fosters a sense of inner peace and contentment that extends far beyond the act of giving itself.

215

F. A Holistic Sense of Success

In the pursuit of financial success, individuals often discover that true fulfillment comes not just from personal achievement, but from making a meaningful difference in the lives of others. Philanthropy complements traditional measures of success, offering a holistic sense of accomplishment.

G. An Enduring Legacy of Joy

The joy generated through philanthropy extends beyond a momentary experience; it becomes an enduring part of your legacy. Your acts of generosity inspire future generations, fostering a culture of giving that perpetuates joy and fulfillment.

2. Connection: Fostering Community and Collaboration

Philanthropy is a powerful catalyst for connection. It brings together individuals, organizations, and communities with shared values and a common purpose. These connections not only amplify the impact of philanthropic efforts but also create a sense of belonging and unity.

A. Building Bridges

Philanthropy builds bridges across diverse backgrounds, beliefs, and experiences. It unites people who might not otherwise have crossed paths, forging connections that transcend societal divisions.

B. Shared Values and Visions

Donors and recipients of philanthropy often share common values and visions. This alignment creates a sense of kinship and reinforces the notion that together, they can drive positive change.

C. Community Engagement

Philanthropy encourages community engagement. It empowers individuals to actively participate in addressing local, national, and global issues. This engagement fosters a sense of ownership and responsibility for the well-being of others.

D. Collaborative Efforts

Philanthropy frequently involves collaborative efforts between donors, nonprofits, government agencies, and community stakeholders. These collaborations bring together diverse perspectives and expertise, leading to more comprehensive and sustainable solutions.

E. Learning and Growth

The connections forged through philanthropy often serve as opportunities for learning and growth. Donors gain insights into the challenges faced by communities and individuals, deepening their understanding of the world and fostering personal growth.

F. A Sense of Belonging

Engaging in philanthropy provides a profound sense of belonging. It creates a network of like-minded individuals and organizations dedicated to creating positive change. This sense of belonging can be a powerful source of support and inspiration.

G. Legacy of Connection

The connections established through philanthropy endure as part of your legacy. They continue to thrive, connecting generations of individuals who share a commitment to making the world a better place.

3. Legacy: Impact That Endures

Philanthropy is a legacy that transcends the boundaries of time and space. It leaves an indelible mark on the world—a legacy of compassion, generosity, and positive change. Here, we explore how philanthropy shapes a lasting legacy that impacts society and future generations.

A. Perpetuating Values

Philanthropy is a means of perpetuating your values, beliefs, and life lessons. It ensures that your principles continue to influence and inspire those who come after you. Your commitment to philanthropy becomes an integral part of your identity, reflecting the values you hold dear and the positive impact you wish to leave on the world.

B. Supporting Loved Ones

One of the most profound aspects of philanthropy is its capacity to support your loved ones, ensuring they have the resources they need to pursue their dreams and aspirations. Your philanthropic efforts can fund educational opportunities, provide financial security, and empower the next generation to thrive.

C. Impacting Causes You Care About

Beyond supporting your family, philanthropy allows you to have a lasting impact on causes and organizations that are close to your heart. Whether you are passionate about education, healthcare, environmental conservation, or social justice, your philanthropic contributions can drive meaningful change in these areas.

D. Leaving a Mark on Society

Philanthropy extends your legacy to society at large. It can fund groundbreaking research that leads to medical advancements, support educational initiatives that empower underserved communities, or address pressing social and environmental challenges. Your philanthropic contributions become a catalyst for positive transformation in the world.

E. Generational Continuity

Philanthropy fosters generational continuity. It instills a sense of responsibility and purpose in your descendants, encouraging them to carry forward your philanthropic legacy. Through shared values and a commitment to giving, your family can have a lasting impact on future generations.

F. A Legacy of Inspiration

Your philanthropic legacy serves as a source of inspiration for others. It demonstrates the profound difference that one individual or family can make in the lives of many. By leaving a legacy of compassion and generosity, you inspire others to embark on their own journeys of philanthropy.

G. Institutional Impact

In some cases, philanthropy leads to the establishment of institutions and foundations dedicated to the causes you care about. These institutions can continue your work long into the future, perpetuating your legacy on a broader scale.

H. Creating a Better World

Ultimately, philanthropy is about creating a better world. It is a testament to the belief that positive change is possible and that each person can contribute to the greater good. Your philanthropic legacy contributes to the collective effort to build a more compassionate, just, and sustainable world for all.

Conclusion: The Transformative Power of Philanthropy

As we conclude this exploration of the transformative power of philanthropy, it becomes evident that philanthropy is not merely an act of giving; it is a profound expression of the human spirit. It embodies empathy, compassion, and a commitment to making the world a better place. Philanthropy touches every facet of human existence—enriching lives, fostering connections, and shaping a legacy that endures.

In the pages of this book, we have journeyed through the principles and practices of philanthropy, from understanding the motivations behind giving to the practical strategies for effective philanthropic endeavors. We have witnessed the impact of philanthropy on individuals, communities, and society as a whole.

As you embark on your own philanthropic journey, remember that philanthropy is not defined by the size of your contributions but by the depth of your commitment to creating positive change. Whether you are starting small or have the means to make substantial gifts, your philanthropic efforts matter. They matter to those you support, to the causes you champion, and to the world that benefits from your generosity.

May this book serve as an inspiration and a guide as you navigate the world of philanthropy. May it empower you to embark on a transformative journey of giving that not only enriches the lives of others but also brings profound fulfillment, connection, and a legacy of positive change to your own life.

In the words of Mahatma Gandhi, "You must be the change you wish to see in the world." Through philanthropy, you can be that change, and in doing so, you can illuminate the path toward a brighter and more compassionate future for all.

Appendix: Resources for Philanthropy

This appendix provides a comprehensive list of resources, organizations, and tools to support your philanthropic journey. Whether you are seeking guidance on effective giving, researching nonprofit organizations, or exploring opportunities for impact, these resources can be valuable companions in your philanthropic endeavors.

A. Philanthropic Organizations and Foundations

1. **The Bill and Melinda Gates Foundation:** A leading global philanthropic organization dedicated to addressing pressing issues, such as global health, poverty alleviation, and education.

2. **The Rockefeller Foundation:** Known for its commitment to improving the well-being of humanity worldwide, with a focus on innovation and resilience.

3. **The Ford Foundation:** A foundation that works to reduce inequality and promote social justice in various areas, including economic opportunity, racial justice, and civic engagement.

4. **The Open Society Foundations:** Founded by George Soros, this organization supports initiatives related to human rights, democracy, and justice around the world.

5. **The Carnegie Corporation of New York:** Focused on advancing education, democracy, and international peace, this foundation has a long history of philanthropy.

6. **The Chan Zuckerberg Initiative:** Established by Mark Zuckerberg and Priscilla Chan, this initiative aims to address

important global challenges through a combination of philanthropy, impact investing, and advocacy.

7. **The MacArthur Foundation:** Known for its "genius grants," this foundation supports creative individuals and innovative projects in various fields.

B. **B. Philanthropic Advisories and Services

1. **Philanthropy Advisors:** Consulting firms and advisors specializing in philanthropy can provide personalized guidance on effective giving strategies, impact assessment, and donor education.

2. **National Philanthropic Trust:** An organization that offers philanthropic solutions, including donor-advised funds and supporting organizations, to facilitate charitable giving.

3. **The Philanthropy Roundtable:** A network of philanthropic organizations and donors that provides resources, research, and best practices in philanthropy.

4. **Exponent Philanthropy:** A membership organization that supports foundations with small staffs and modest budgets, offering resources and networking opportunities.

5. **Bridgespan Group:** A nonprofit consulting firm that partners with mission-driven organizations and philanthropists to accelerate social change.

C. Research and Information

1. **GuideStar:** A comprehensive database of nonprofit organizations, providing financial information, programmatic details, and reviews from donors and volunteers.

2. **Charity Navigator:** An online platform that evaluates and rates nonprofit organizations based on their financial health, accountability, and transparency.

3. **Philanthropy News Digest:** A service of the Foundation Center, this platform offers news, RFPs (requests for proposals), and other resources related to philanthropy.

4. **Center for Effective Philanthropy:** A research and advisory organization that focuses on improving the impact of philanthropic efforts through assessments and best practices.

5. **Giving Compass:** An online resource center that curates articles, tools, and insights to help donors make informed decisions about their giving.

6. **The Chronicle of Philanthropy:** A publication covering news and trends in the philanthropic sector.

D. Impact Assessment and Evaluation Tools

1. **ImpactMatters:** An organization that assesses the cost-effectiveness of nonprofits and provides impact estimates for donors.

2. **Social Impact Exchange:** A platform that connects donors with high-impact nonprofit organizations and offers resources on effective giving.

3. **The Stanford Social Innovation Review:** A publication that explores best practices in social innovation and impact measurement.

4. **Giving What We Can:** An organization that encourages individuals to pledge a portion of their income to effective

charities and provides impact calculators to assess giving effectiveness.

E. Community Foundations

1. **Silicon Valley Community Foundation:** One of the largest community foundations in the United States, serving donors and nonprofits in the Silicon Valley region.

2. **The Chicago Community Trust:** A community foundation dedicated to improving the Chicago metropolitan area through strategic philanthropy.

3. **New York Community Trust:** One of the oldest and largest community foundations, serving the New York City area.

4. **The Cleveland Foundation:** The first community foundation in the world, committed to enhancing the quality of life in Greater Cleveland.

F. Global Philanthropy

1. **GlobalGiving:** An online platform that connects donors with grassroots projects around the world, allowing donors to support causes they are passionate about globally.

2. **Charities Aid Foundation (CAF):** A global organization that helps individuals and businesses support charitable causes worldwide.

3. **GiveWell:** A nonprofit organization that conducts in-depth research to identify highly effective charities and provides recommendations for donors.

4. **Effective Altruism:** A movement focused on using evidence and reason to make the world a better place, often through strategic philanthropy.

G. Philanthropy Education and Networks

1. **The Lilly Family School of Philanthropy:** The world's first school dedicated to the study and teaching of philanthropy.

2. **The Philanthropy Workshop:** An organization that provides education and networking opportunities for philanthropists to maximize their impact.

3. **Young Philanthropy:** A network of young philanthropists and social investors dedicated to making a positive impact.

4. **ExO Philanthropy:** An initiative focused on leveraging exponential technologies and innovation for social impact.

H. Legal and Financial Advisors

1. **Philanthropic Legal Advisors:** Attorneys specializing in philanthropic law can assist with estate planning, establishing foundations, and structuring charitable gifts.

2. **Certified Financial Planners (CFPs):** Financial advisors with expertise in philanthropic planning can help individuals and families align their financial goals with charitable giving strategies.

I. Government Resources

1. **Internal Revenue Service (IRS):** Information on tax regulations related to charitable giving, including deductions and requirements for tax-exempt organizations.

2. **The Catalog of Federal Domestic Assistance (CFDA):** A government-wide compendium of federal programs, projects, services, and activities that provide assistance or benefits to the American public.

These resources are invaluable tools on your philanthropic journey. Whether you are starting your philanthropic endeavors or looking to enhance your impact, these organizations, platforms, and services can guide and support your efforts to create positive change in the world.

Impactful Stories of Giving

Let's delve into stories of individuals who have made a meaningful impact through their wealth and philanthropy, inspiring us to consider our own potential for positive change:

Case Study 1: The Education Champion - John's Scholarship Foundation

John had always been a firm believer in the power of education to transform lives. His own journey from a modest upbringing to a successful entrepreneur had highlighted the role education played in his personal growth and success. As he looked around his community, he saw countless bright young minds who lacked access to quality education due to financial constraints. This realization stirred something within him, a deep desire to make a difference.

The Birth of the Scholarship Foundation:

John's philanthropic journey began with a simple idea: to establish a scholarship foundation dedicated to providing underprivileged youth access to quality education. He believed that education was not just a ticket to personal growth but also a key to breaking the cycle of poverty in underserved communities.

To turn his vision into reality, John enlisted the help of education experts, financial advisors, and legal professionals. Together, they developed a comprehensive plan for the foundation, outlining its mission, governance structure, and operational guidelines. John was determined to ensure that the foundation would operate efficiently, maximizing its impact.

Fundraising and Partnerships:

Launching the foundation required significant financial resources. John, with his business acumen and network, started by making a substantial personal donation. He also reached out to his business contacts, friends, and family, encouraging them to join him in supporting the cause. John's genuine passion and commitment were contagious, and soon, he had a group of dedicated donors backing the foundation.

To expand the foundation's reach, John actively sought partnerships with local schools, colleges, and educational organizations. These partnerships allowed the foundation to identify deserving students and ensure that the scholarships reached those who needed them the most. The foundation also collaborated with educators to provide mentorship and guidance to scholarship recipients, recognizing that financial support alone was not enough to ensure their success.

Transforming Lives, One Scholarship at a Time:

As the scholarship foundation gained momentum, it began awarding scholarships to underprivileged students. The impact was immediate and profound. John received letters and testimonials from scholarship recipients expressing their gratitude and sharing their dreams of pursuing higher education. Many of these students were the first in their families to attend college, breaking barriers and setting an example for their communities.

Over the years, the foundation expanded its programs and outreach, reaching students in various regions and supporting a wide range of educational pursuits. It wasn't just about funding tuition fees; the foundation also offered scholarships for extracurricular activities, vocational training, and even entrepreneurship programs.

Measuring Impact and Continuous Improvement:

John was committed to ensuring that the foundation's efforts were making a genuine impact. He established rigorous monitoring and evaluation processes to track the progress of scholarship recipients. This data-driven approach allowed the foundation to continuously refine its programs and adapt to the evolving needs of the students it served.

The foundation's success also attracted the attention of other philanthropists and organizations. John was invited to speak at conferences and share his experiences in philanthropy. He used these platforms to advocate for increased support for education and encouraged others to join the cause.

Legacy and Future Generations:

As John grew older, he knew that he wanted his foundation's work to continue long after he was gone. He engaged his family in discussions about the foundation's future, involving them in its governance and decision-making. Together, they created a robust succession plan, ensuring that the scholarship foundation would remain a force for good for generations to come.

John's legacy extended far beyond the scholarships themselves. His dedication to education had a ripple effect, inspiring young minds to dream big and pursue their goals. The foundation became a beacon of hope for underprivileged youth, a testament to the transformative power of education.

Case Study 2: The Environmental Steward - Susan's Conservation Legacy

Susan had always felt a deep connection to the natural world. Her childhood was filled with outdoor adventures, from camping in national parks to exploring pristine beaches. As she grew older, she became increasingly aware of the environmental challenges facing the planet. It was this awareness that led her to dedicate a significant portion of her wealth to environmental conservation.

Early Life and Passion for Nature:

Susan's love for nature was cultivated during her early years, thanks to her parents' commitment to environmental stewardship. They instilled in her a deep respect for the Earth and a sense of responsibility to protect it. As she pursued her education and career, Susan kept her passion for the environment alive, frequently volunteering for conservation organizations and participating in local clean-up efforts.

Building Wealth and Philanthropic Vision:

Susan's career in finance proved to be successful, allowing her to accumulate considerable wealth. Throughout her journey, she remained committed to her environmental values. She attended conferences on conservation, read extensively on environmental issues, and actively engaged with environmental organizations.

It was during one such conference that Susan was struck by a presentation on the rapid decline of certain endangered species. The urgency of the situation hit home, and she knew she had to do more to protect the natural world she cherished. This marked the beginning of her philanthropic journey.

The Birth of the Conservation Foundation:

Susan decided to establish a conservation foundation dedicated to preserving endangered habitats and restoring ecosystems. She believed that her wealth could be a force for positive change in the world. With the guidance of experts in conservation biology and environmental policy, she formulated a clear mission for her foundation: to protect biodiversity and ensure a sustainable future for the planet.

Strategic Grantmaking and Partnerships:

One of the key principles Susan adopted was a strategic approach to grantmaking. She didn't want her foundation's efforts to be scattered; she wanted every dollar to have a meaningful impact. To achieve this, Susan and her team conducted thorough research to identify projects and organizations with a track record of successful conservation work.

The foundation formed partnerships with established environmental NGOs, collaborating on initiatives that aligned with its mission. These partnerships allowed Susan's foundation to leverage the expertise and resources of larger organizations while maintaining a focused approach to impact.

Protecting Biodiversity:

The foundation's work encompassed a wide range of projects, from protecting vital rainforests in South America to conserving critical marine habitats. Susan's commitment to preserving biodiversity extended to supporting scientific research, funding anti-poaching efforts, and advocating for policies that safeguarded endangered species.

Restoration and Sustainable Practices:

Susan recognized the importance of not only preserving existing habitats but also restoring degraded ecosystems. Her foundation funded projects focused on reforestation, wetland restoration, and sustainable agriculture. These initiatives aimed to reverse environmental damage and promote practices that would benefit both the planet and local communities.

Education and Outreach:

Susan believed that raising awareness about environmental issues was essential to driving change. Her foundation invested in educational programs that taught communities about the importance of conservation and the value of biodiversity. These programs empowered individuals to take action in their own lives and advocate for environmental protection.

In addition to local outreach, Susan's foundation supported documentaries, publications, and campaigns that highlighted pressing environmental challenges. By harnessing the power of media and storytelling, they aimed to reach a global audience and inspire collective action.

Long-Term Commitment:

Susan's approach to philanthropy was characterized by a long-term commitment to the causes she cared about deeply. She understood that environmental conservation was not a short-term endeavor but a lifelong mission. To ensure the sustainability of her foundation's work, she established an endowment fund, ensuring that it would continue to support conservation efforts for generations.

Collaborative Leadership:

As Susan grew older, she knew that her foundation's success would depend on a strong team and clear leadership succession. She actively involved her family in the foundation's work, fostering a sense of shared purpose and commitment to the cause. Her children and grandchildren participated in foundation activities and were encouraged to take on leadership roles.

A Lasting Legacy:

Susan's dedication to environmental stewardship left an indelible mark on the world. Her foundation's work had a tangible impact on preserving biodiversity, restoring ecosystems, and advocating for a sustainable future. It became a symbol of what could be achieved when passion, resources, and strategic philanthropy converged.

Case Study 3: The Healthcare Philanthropist - David's Medical Clinic

David had dedicated his life to the practice of medicine. As a physician, he had witnessed firsthand the importance of access to quality healthcare. However, he was acutely aware of the healthcare disparities that plagued underserved communities. When he retired from his medical practice, he decided to take action and address this issue directly.

Early Medical Career and Compassion:

David's journey in medicine had been driven by a deep sense of compassion. He had chosen to specialize in family medicine because he believed in the power of preventive care and building strong patient-doctor relationships. Over the years, he had served in various medical capacities, from community clinics to volunteer missions in remote areas.

The Idea of the Medical Clinic:

232

Upon retiring, David couldn't shake the feeling that he had more to give. He knew that many underserved communities lacked access to basic healthcare services, and this inequity troubled him. It was during a visit to a free clinic in a disadvantaged neighborhood that the idea struck him: he could establish a medical clinic that provided comprehensive healthcare services to those in need.

Creating a Vision:

David's vision for the medical clinic was clear. He wanted to create a welcoming and inclusive space where individuals and families could receive high-quality healthcare regardless of their financial situation. He envisioned a clinic that offered primary care, preventive services, dental care, and access to specialists—all under one roof.

Building the Foundation:

Turning his vision into reality required careful planning and significant financial investment. David enlisted the help of fellow healthcare professionals, including nurses, dentists, and specialists, who shared his passion for serving the underserved. Together, they formed the core team that would bring the medical clinic to life.

Securing Funding and Community Support:

To fund the clinic's construction and ongoing operations, David reached out to his professional network, former colleagues, and local philanthropists. He also organized fundraisers and sought grants from foundations dedicated to healthcare access. The response was overwhelmingly positive, with many individuals and organizations eager to support the clinic's mission.

Locating in an Underserved Community:

David's team identified an underserved community where the clinic's impact would be most significant. They secured a centrally located building and began renovating it to meet the healthcare needs of the community. David made sure that the clinic was easily accessible by public transportation, ensuring that transportation barriers wouldn't hinder access to care.

Comprehensive Care and Holistic Approach:

When the clinic opened its doors, it offered a comprehensive range of healthcare services, from routine check-ups to specialized treatments. David emphasized a holistic approach to healthcare, focusing not just on treating illnesses but also on preventive care and patient education.

Collaboration with Community Organizations:

Recognizing that healthcare was just one aspect of overall well-being, David's clinic forged partnerships with local social service organizations. This allowed them to connect patients with resources for housing, food security, mental health support, and job training. The clinic became a hub for holistic care and community support.

Patient-Centered Care:

At the heart of the clinic's success was its patient-centered approach. David and his team prioritized building trusting relationships with patients, taking the time to understand their individual needs and circumstances. This approach led to better health outcomes and empowered patients to take control of their health.

A Lifelong Commitment:

David's commitment to the clinic extended well beyond its opening. Even in retirement, he remained actively involved, volunteering his medical expertise and mentoring young healthcare professionals. He also encouraged the clinic's team to stay true to its mission and maintain the highest standards of care.

Legacy of Compassion:

David's medical clinic became a beacon of hope for the community it served. It provided healthcare and support to thousands of individuals who had previously struggled to access medical services. David's legacy was one of compassion, dedication, and a profound impact on the health and well-being of those in need.

These case studies illustrate the transformative power of philanthropy and the ability of individuals to make a lasting impact on the world. John, Susan, and David each dedicated themselves to causes they were passionate about, leveraging their resources and expertise to effect positive change. Their stories serve as an inspiration to others, demonstrating that with vision, commitment, and strategic philanthropy, anyone can leave a lasting legacy of compassion and social impact.

Enriching Lives and Leaving a Mark

Legacy and philanthropy are the final chapters of the wealth mastery journey—a journey that transcends personal wealth and financial achievements. Leaving a legacy is about enriching lives, preserving values, and making a lasting mark on the world. Philanthropy, in all its forms, allows us to give back, spread positivity, and contribute to the betterment of society.

As you contemplate your legacy and philanthropic endeavors, remember that it's not the size of your contribution that matters most, but the sincerity and intention behind it. Your legacy and acts of kindness have the power to ripple through time, inspiring others to follow in your footsteps and make the world a better place.

Chapter 9: Navigating Economic Challenges

In our pursuit of wealth mastery, it's crucial to recognize that the path to financial success is not always smooth. Economic downturns, recessions, and financial setbacks are part of the financial landscape. However, what truly matters is how we navigate and overcome these challenges. In this chapter, we will address the impact of economic downturns and provide strategies for resilience and recovery during tough times. Through real-life stories of individuals who thrived despite adversity, we will uncover the resilience and determination that can lead to financial triumph even in the face of economic challenges.

The Reality of Economic Challenges

Economic challenges, such as recessions and financial setbacks, can be daunting. They can disrupt financial stability, erode savings, and create uncertainty. Understanding their potential impact is the first step toward effectively navigating these challenges:

Navigating Financial Challenges: Strategies for Uncertain Times

Life is filled with financial uncertainties, and it's essential to be prepared for unexpected challenges that can impact your financial well-being. Whether it's a recession, a sudden job loss, or economic uncertainty, having a plan in place can help you weather the storm and emerge stronger. In this chapter, we'll explore various strategies for navigating these financial challenges and securing your financial future.

1. Recessions: Riding the Economic Waves

Recessions are a recurring feature of the economic landscape. They are characterized by a contraction in economic activity, rising unemployment, and financial market volatility. While recessions are challenging, they are also a natural part of the economic cycle. Here's how you can navigate them effectively:

Understanding Recessions:

Recessions are typically caused by a variety of factors, including a decline in consumer spending, reduced business investment, or external shocks like a financial crisis or a global pandemic. Understanding the root causes can help you anticipate and prepare for economic downturns.

Building Emergency Savings:

One of the best defenses against recessions is a robust emergency fund. Aim to save at least three to six months' worth of living expenses in a liquid savings account. This cushion can help you cover essential expenses in case of job loss or reduced income during a recession.

Diversifying Investments:

During economic downturns, financial markets can experience significant volatility. Diversifying your investment portfolio across various asset classes, such as stocks, bonds, and real estate, can help spread risk and reduce the impact of market fluctuations.

Reducing Debt:

Lowering high-interest debt levels before a recession hits can free up more of your income during challenging times. Prioritize paying off credit card debt and consider consolidating loans to reduce interest costs.

Leveraging Government Assistance:

During recessions, governments often implement stimulus programs and relief measures to support individuals and businesses. Stay informed about available assistance programs and consider utilizing them if necessary.

2. Financial Setbacks: Bouncing Back from Unexpected Challenges

Life is unpredictable, and financial setbacks can occur when you least expect them. Whether it's a sudden medical emergency, job loss, or unexpected expenses, here's how to recover and regain financial stability:

Creating a Contingency Plan:

Prepare for unforeseen circumstances by creating a contingency plan. Identify potential risks, such as health issues or job instability, and outline steps you would take to address them. Having a plan in place can reduce anxiety during difficult times.

Insurance Coverage:

Insurance can be a valuable safety net. Ensure you have adequate health, disability, and life insurance coverage. These policies can provide financial support when you need it most.

Emergency Fund:

Maintain an emergency fund to cover unexpected expenses. Ideally, your emergency fund should cover three to six months' worth of living expenses. If you've depleted it due to a setback, prioritize rebuilding it as soon as possible.

Job Loss Recovery:

If you lose your job, take immediate steps to secure your finances. Apply for unemployment benefits if eligible, create a revised budget, and explore alternative income sources such as part-time work or freelance opportunities.

Seeking Professional Advice:

Consider consulting a financial advisor or counselor to help you navigate through financial setbacks. They can provide guidance on budgeting, debt management, and investment decisions tailored to your specific situation.

3. Economic Uncertainty: Mastering Financial Flexibility

Economic uncertainty can make financial planning feel like navigating uncharted waters. However, by mastering financial flexibility and adaptability, you can better prepare for the unknown:

Flexible Budgeting:

During periods of economic uncertainty, it's crucial to have a flexible budget. Create a budget that allows for adjustments in response to changing circumstances. Prioritize essential expenses, but be ready to cut back on non-essential spending when needed.

Enhanced Savings:

Bolster your savings during times of economic uncertainty. Consider temporarily directing more of your income into savings and investments, building a financial buffer to weather potential storms.

Risk Assessment:

Review your investment portfolio regularly and assess your risk tolerance. Make necessary adjustments to align your investments with your comfort level and long-term financial goals.

Multiple Income Streams:

Diversifying your income sources can enhance your financial stability during uncertain times. Explore opportunities for side hustles, freelance work, or passive income streams to supplement your primary income.

Continuous Learning:

Stay informed about economic trends, job market dynamics, and investment opportunities. Continuous learning and adaptability are valuable assets when navigating economic uncertainty.

While financial challenges and economic uncertainties are inevitable, being prepared and having a plan in place can make a significant difference. By understanding the nature of recessions, creating contingency plans, and mastering financial flexibility, you can navigate through uncertain times with confidence and resilience. Remember that your financial journey is a marathon, not a sprint, and being prepared for the long haul is the key to success.

Strategies for Resilience and Recovery

While economic challenges can be formidable, resilience and recovery are possible with the right strategies and mindset. Here are strategies to navigate economic challenges effectively:

Mastering Financial Resilience: Strategies for Unpredictable Times

Financial resilience is the ability to withstand and recover from financial setbacks and challenges. It's a crucial aspect of financial well-being, as life often throws unexpected curveballs. Whether it's a sudden job loss, a medical emergency, or economic uncertainty, having a resilient financial foundation can make all the difference. In this chapter, we'll explore seven key strategies to master financial resilience.

1. Emergency Fund: Your Financial Safety Net

An emergency fund is your first line of defense against financial crises. It's a pool of money set aside to cover unexpected expenses, such as medical bills, car repairs, or unforeseen job loss. Having an emergency fund can provide peace of mind and financial security during turbulent times.

Building and Maintaining Your Emergency Fund:

- Aim to save at least three to six months' worth of living expenses in your emergency fund. The exact amount depends on your individual circumstances and risk tolerance.
- Start by creating a budget and identifying areas where you can cut expenses to allocate more funds toward your emergency fund.
- Consider setting up a dedicated savings account for your emergency fund to prevent the temptation of dipping into it for non-urgent expenses.
- Regularly review and replenish your emergency fund, especially after using it for unexpected costs.

2. Diversified Investments: Strengthening Your Financial Portfolio

Diversification is a fundamental principle of investing. It involves spreading your investments across a range of asset classes, industries, and geographic regions. A diversified portfolio is less vulnerable to market volatility and can better withstand economic downturns.

The Benefits of Diversification:

- Reduces the impact of poor performance in a single asset or sector.
- Provides the potential for more consistent returns over the long term.
- Enhances overall portfolio stability by balancing risk and reward.

Building a Diversified Portfolio:

- Invest in a mix of asset classes, including stocks, bonds, real estate, and alternative investments.
- Consider diversifying within asset classes by choosing different industries and geographic regions.
- Regularly review and rebalance your portfolio to maintain your desired asset allocation.

3. Debt Management: Lightening the Financial Burden

Debt can be a heavy burden during challenging times. High-interest debts, such as credit card balances, can quickly erode your financial stability. Prioritizing debt reduction can provide financial relief and flexibility.

Steps to Effective Debt Management:

- Start by creating a comprehensive list of all your outstanding debts, including balances and interest rates.
- Prioritize high-interest debts for repayment, allocating extra funds to pay them off more quickly.
- Consider debt consolidation options, such as balance transfer credit cards or personal loans, to lower interest costs.

- Avoid accumulating new debt during challenging times and practice responsible spending.

4. Budget and Expense Management: Navigating Financial Storms

Creating and adhering to a budget is a cornerstone of financial resilience. A well-structured budget helps you identify essential expenses, prioritize spending, and cut back on non-essential items when necessary.

Budgeting Tips for Uncertain Times:

- Develop a detailed budget that includes all sources of income and categorizes expenses.
- Clearly distinguish between essential expenses (e.g., housing, utilities, groceries) and discretionary spending (e.g., entertainment, dining out).
- Focus on essentials during periods of economic uncertainty, allocating the majority of your income to these categories.
- Regularly review and adjust your budget as your financial situation changes.

5. Continuous Learning: Investing in Your Future

In a rapidly evolving job market, continuous learning is essential. It enhances your employability and equips you with the skills needed to adapt to changing circumstances. Lifelong learning is an investment in your career resilience.

Strategies for Lifelong Learning:

- Identify areas where you can enhance your skills, whether through formal education, online courses, or self-study.

- Stay informed about industry trends and developments by reading relevant publications and attending conferences or webinars.
- Seek mentorship or guidance from experienced professionals in your field.
- Be open to acquiring new skills or exploring different career paths when necessary.

6. Flexibility: Adapting to Changing Circumstances

Flexibility is a key trait of financially resilient individuals. It involves being open to adjusting your financial plans and goals when faced with unexpected challenges or opportunities.

Embracing Financial Flexibility:

- Recognize that life rarely follows a linear path, and be prepared to pivot when necessary.
- Regularly review your financial goals and priorities to ensure they align with your current circumstances and values.
- Consider alternative income sources or side hustles to supplement your primary income.
- Be open to adjusting your investment strategy or risk tolerance based on changing market conditions.

7. Professional Advice: A Guiding Light in Tough Times

During difficult financial periods, seeking guidance from financial advisors or professionals can be invaluable. They can provide expert insights, help you make informed decisions, and offer emotional support.

When to Seek Professional Advice:

- When facing complex financial decisions, such as estate planning or retirement strategies.

- After a significant life event, such as marriage, divorce, or the birth of a child.
- During periods of financial distress, job loss, or market volatility.
- To create a long-term financial plan tailored to your goals and circumstances.

Financial resilience is not about avoiding challenges; it's about preparing for them. By building an emergency fund, diversifying investments, managing debt, budgeting wisely, investing in continuous learning, embracing flexibility, and seeking professional advice, you can strengthen your financial foundation. Remember that financial resilience is a journey, and each step you take brings you closer to a more secure and adaptable financial future.

Stories of Triumph Over Adversity

To illustrate the power of resilience and determination in overcoming economic challenges, let's delve into real-life stories of individuals who thrived despite adversity:

Case Study 1: The Entrepreneurial Spirit - Sarah's Triumph Over Financial Setbacks

Sarah's story is a testament to the resilience and determination of the entrepreneurial spirit. During the 2008 recession, she faced severe financial setbacks that threatened the very existence of her business. It was a challenging time for entrepreneurs worldwide, with economic turbulence affecting businesses of all sizes. However, Sarah's unwavering dedication and strategic thinking enabled her not only to survive but to thrive in the face of adversity.

The Prelude: The Entrepreneurial Dream

Before the recession hit, Sarah had built a successful business. Her entrepreneurial journey had begun years earlier when she identified a gap in the market for unique, handcrafted furniture. Her passion for woodworking and her vision for creating bespoke pieces had driven her to start her own business. Sarah's products had gained a loyal customer base, and her brand was well-regarded in her community.

The Storm Clouds Gather: The Impact of the 2008 Recession

The 2008 recession, triggered by the global financial crisis, brought a wave of economic uncertainty and turmoil. Consumer spending plummeted, and businesses across various industries suffered. Sarah's business was not immune to these challenges. As the recession took hold, her customer base dwindled, and orders for her custom furniture pieces dwindled.

Additionally, Sarah had taken out a loan to expand her business just before the recession hit. The timing could not have been worse. The combination of reduced sales and the burden of loan repayments pushed her into a dire financial situation. Debt began to accumulate, and Sarah faced mounting pressure to keep her business afloat.

The Turning Point: Reevaluating the Business Model

Rather than succumbing to despair, Sarah decided to confront the challenges head-on. She knew that resilience was a crucial trait for entrepreneurs, and she was determined to persevere. Her first step was to reevaluate her business model. Sarah understood that she needed to adapt to the changing market conditions to survive.

She began by identifying the aspects of her business that were still viable and in demand. Although large custom furniture orders had slowed, she noticed an uptick in demand for smaller, more affordable pieces. Recognizing this shift in consumer behavior,

Sarah adjusted her product offerings accordingly. She started creating a line of smaller, ready-made furniture items that catered to this new demand.

A Focus on Efficiency and Cost Reduction

Sarah also scrutinized her business operations for areas where she could reduce costs without compromising quality. She found ways to streamline production processes, negotiate better deals with suppliers, and minimize overhead expenses. These cost-saving measures helped her preserve her business's financial stability.

Connecting with Customers: Building Loyalty

To reconnect with her customer base and rebuild trust, Sarah increased her efforts in customer engagement and satisfaction. She reached out to past clients and offered special promotions on her new product line. By showing appreciation for their continued support, she was able to maintain a loyal customer base.

Hard Work and Perseverance: The Road to Recovery

Sarah's journey was not without challenges and sleepless nights. The weight of debt and the uncertainty of the market weighed heavily on her. But her determination and belief in her business kept her going. She worked tirelessly, often putting in long hours to meet orders and handle the day-to-day operations.

Gradually, her efforts began to pay off. Sales of her smaller, more affordable furniture pieces started to climb, providing a lifeline for her business. As the economy slowly recovered, consumer confidence improved, and Sarah's business regained its footing.

Triumph Over Adversity: A Thriving Business

Over time, Sarah's business not only recovered but thrived. Her adaptability and resilience in the face of financial setbacks had not only saved her enterprise but also positioned it for future success. Her willingness to evolve her business model, focus on efficiency, and maintain a strong connection with her customers had been instrumental in her turnaround.

Sarah's story serves as a powerful reminder that entrepreneurship is not without its challenges, but with determination and strategic thinking, one can overcome even the most formidable obstacles. Her journey through the recession had not only preserved her business but also reinforced her belief in the entrepreneurial spirit's power to triumph over adversity.

Case Study 2: The Job Seeker's Journey - Mike's Resilience Amid Economic Turmoil

Mike's story is a testament to the resilience and adaptability of individuals in the face of job loss and economic uncertainty. The global financial crisis of 2008 led to widespread job cuts and hiring freezes across various industries, leaving many talented professionals like Mike without stable employment. However, Mike's determination, proactive approach, and commitment to self-improvement ultimately led him to new opportunities and a brighter career path.

The Prelude: A Promising Career

Before the economic downturn, Mike had established himself as a highly skilled professional in the finance sector. He had steadily climbed the corporate ladder, securing a well-paying job with a reputable financial institution. Like many others, he believed that his career trajectory was secure, unaware of the storm that lay ahead.

The Storm Clouds Gather: Job Loss in the Financial Crisis

The 2008 financial crisis sent shockwaves throughout the global economy. Banks and financial institutions were among them hardest hit, with many facing insurmountable challenges. Mike's employer, a prominent investment firm, was no exception. As the crisis deepened, the company was forced to make tough decisions, including layoffs and cost-cutting measures.

Mike found himself caught in the crossfire of these corporate decisions. Despite his exemplary performance and dedication, he received the dreaded news that his position was being eliminated due to restructuring. It was a devastating blow, and he suddenly found himself facing an uncertain future.

The Turning Point: A Proactive Approach to Job Seeker's Journey

Rather than succumbing to despair, Mike decided to take a proactive approach to his situation. He recognized that the job market was highly competitive and that he needed to set himself apart from other job seekers. Here are some key steps he took:

1. Skills Enhancement: Mike identified areas where he could enhance his skills and increase his employability. He enrolled in relevant courses and certifications, focusing on emerging trends and technologies in his industry. This commitment to continuous learning allowed him to stay competitive in a rapidly changing job market.

2. Networking: Recognizing the value of connections in the job market, Mike devoted time to building and expanding his professional network. He attended industry events, joined online forums and LinkedIn groups, and reached out to former colleagues and mentors. Networking provided him with valuable insights, job leads, and a support system during his job search.

3. Tailored Resumes and Cover Letters: Mike understood the importance of customizing his application materials for each job opportunity. He meticulously crafted tailored resumes and cover letters that highlighted his skills, achievements, and alignment with the specific role and company. This personalized approach increased his chances of standing out to potential employers.

4. Interview Preparation: Mike invested time in interview preparation, researching companies, practicing responses to common interview questions, and refining his interview skills. This preparation ensured that he was confident and well-prepared when meeting with potential employers.

5. Contract Work: Recognizing that full-time positions were scarce, Mike explored contract and freelance opportunities in his field. These short-term projects provided valuable experience, allowed him to showcase his skills, and generated income during his job search.

The Triumph: A New Opportunity

Mike's journey through the job market was not without its challenges. He faced rejection and uncertainty along the way. However, his resilience, combined with his proactive approach, eventually led to a breakthrough. He secured a contract position with a forward-thinking startup that recognized his skills and potential.

This initial contract role served as a stepping stone to a permanent position with the company. Not only did Mike regain his professional stability, but he also found himself in a role that offered greater career growth potential and alignment with his long-term goals.

Case Study 3: The Investment Recovery - James' Patience Amid Market Volatility

James' story is a testament to the importance of patience and a long-term investment strategy when navigating market volatility. Like many investors, he experienced significant losses during a stock market crash, which could have easily led to panic-selling and irreversible financial setbacks. However, James chose to take a disciplined and patient approach to his investments, ultimately not only recovering his losses but also achieving substantial gains.

The Prelude: A Savvy Investor's Portfolio

Before the stock market crash, James had diligently built a well-balanced investment portfolio. He had diversified his investments across various asset classes, including stocks, bonds, and real estate. His investment strategy was grounded in a long-term perspective, and he had a clear financial goal: to secure his retirement and build wealth over time.

The Storm Clouds Gather: The Stock Market Crash

The stock market crash of 2008 brought widespread panic and uncertainty to the investment world. Stock prices plummeted, and many investors faced significant paper losses. James was no exception. The value of his stock holdings declined considerably, and the overall market sentiment was grim.

The Turning Point: A Long-Term Perspective

Amid the market turmoil, James made a crucial decision: he would maintain a long-term perspective and stay committed to his investment strategy. He understood that market fluctuations were a natural part of the investment landscape and that emotional reactions could lead to poor financial decisions.

Rather than succumbing to panic and selling his investments at a loss, James chose to hold onto his diversified portfolio. He continued to contribute to his investments regularly, taking advantage of the lower stock prices to accumulate more shares. This disciplined approach was a reflection of his confidence in the resilience of financial markets over the long term.

The Triumph: Recovery and Substantial Gains

James' patience and commitment to his investment strategy paid off over time. As the years passed, the stock market rebounded, and the value of his investments began to recover. Not only did he recoup the losses incurred during the crash, but he also saw substantial gains as the markets continued to grow.

This experience reinforced James' belief in the power of a well-diversified, long-term investment strategy. He had weathered the storm of market volatility and emerged with a stronger and more prosperous portfolio. His story serves as a reminder that, in the world of investments, patience and discipline can be powerful allies in achieving long-term financial goals.

These case studies exemplify the resilience, determination, and strategic thinking that individuals can employ in the face of financial setbacks and economic challenges. Whether it's an entrepreneur adapting to changing market conditions, a job seeker navigating a tough employment landscape, or an investor withstanding market volatility, these stories showcase the power of perseverance, adaptability, and long-term vision.

** Triumphing Over Adversity**

Economic challenges are an inevitable part of the financial journey, but they need not define our financial future. With resilience, strategic planning, and determination, it's possible to navigate economic downturns, overcome setbacks, and emerge stronger and wiser. The stories of individuals who triumphed over adversity serve as inspiring reminders that challenges can be opportunities for growth and success.

As you continue your journey to wealth mastery, remember that financial resilience is not just about weathering storms but emerging from them with newfound strength. With the right mindset and strategies, you can navigate economic challenges and continue on your path to financial prosperity.

In the chapters that follow, we will delve into advanced wealth-building strategies and financial concepts, equipping you with the knowledge and tools to continue your journey to wealth mastery.

Chapter 10: Wealth Maintenance and Longevity

As we approach the culmination of our journey to wealth mastery, it's essential to recognize that the true test of financial success lies not just in accumulation but in the ability to maintain and grow wealth over time. In this chapter, we will emphasize the importance of wealth maintenance and longevity. We'll offer guidance on essential aspects such as estate planning, retirement, and generational wealth transfer. By sharing insights into preserving wealth for future generations, we'll explore how you can leave a lasting financial legacy.

The Ongoing Commitment to Wealth

Wealth mastery is not a destination; it's an ongoing commitment to nurturing and safeguarding your financial well-being. Here's why wealth maintenance and longevity are paramount:

1. Ensuring Financial Security Through Wealth Maintenance

Financial security is a fundamental aspect of wealth management and maintenance. It encompasses the ability to maintain a comfortable and stress-free lifestyle, even in the face of unexpected challenges, retirement, or economic downturns. Ensuring financial security requires careful planning, disciplined financial management, and a long-term perspective.

The Importance of Financial Security

Financial security is the cornerstone of a worry-free and fulfilling life. It provides peace of mind, knowing that you have the resources to meet your financial needs and objectives. Whether it's covering everyday expenses, funding your children's education, or enjoying a comfortable retirement, financial security underpins all aspects of your financial well-being.

Here are key elements of ensuring financial security through wealth maintenance:

A. Adequate Emergency Fund: An emergency fund is a crucial component of financial security. It serves as a financial cushion that covers unexpected expenses, such as medical emergencies, car repairs, or job loss. A well-funded emergency fund typically holds three to six months' worth of living expenses, providing a safety net during times of financial uncertainty.

B. Debt Management: Effective debt management is integral to financial security. Minimizing high-interest debts, such as credit card balances or personal loans, reduces the financial burden and frees up resources for saving and investing. A lower debt burden also reduces the risk of financial setbacks.

C. Diversified Investments: Wealth maintenance involves preserving and growing your assets over time. Diversifying your investment portfolio across various asset classes, such as stocks, bonds, real estate, and alternative investments, helps spread risk and increase the likelihood of achieving your financial goals. A diversified portfolio is more resilient to market fluctuations.

D. Retirement Planning: Preparing for retirement is a key aspect of financial security. Contributing regularly to retirement accounts, such as 401(k)s or IRAs, ensures that you have a reliable source of income in your post-working years. It's essential to calculate your retirement needs and make adjustments to your savings and investment strategies accordingly.

E. Insurance Coverage: Adequate insurance coverage plays a vital role in financial security. Health insurance, life insurance, disability insurance, and property insurance protect you and your family from unexpected financial burdens. Ensuring that you have the right coverage and reviewing it periodically is essential.

F. Estate Planning: Estate planning is a crucial component of financial security, especially for passing on wealth to loved ones. Establishing a comprehensive estate plan, including wills, trusts, and powers of attorney, ensures that your assets are distributed according to your wishes and minimizes potential estate taxes.

2. Legacy Continuation: Perpetuating Your Impact Beyond Your Lifetime

Effective wealth management goes beyond ensuring your financial security during your lifetime; it allows you to leave a lasting legacy that continues to benefit your loved ones and charitable causes long after you're gone. Legacy continuation is about preserving and extending the impact of your wealth, values, and principles.

A. Supporting Loved Ones: One of the most common motivations for legacy planning is the desire to provide financial support and security to your family and loved ones. Through wealth maintenance and prudent estate planning, you can ensure that your heirs receive inheritances that enable them to achieve their goals, whether it's pursuing higher education, starting a business, or buying a home.

B. Charitable Giving: Many individuals are passionate about supporting charitable causes and making a positive difference in their communities and the world. Wealth maintenance allows you to contribute to these causes during your lifetime and continue your philanthropic efforts through legacy gifts in your estate plan. By designating charitable organizations as beneficiaries or establishing charitable foundations, you can leave a lasting impact on causes that matter to you.

C. Education and Empowerment: Legacy continuation also involves empowering future generations with financial education and resources. By establishing educational funds, scholarships, or financial literacy programs in your estate plan, you can help equip your descendants with the knowledge and tools they need to make sound financial decisions and achieve their aspirations.

D. Values and Principles: Wealth preservation enables you to perpetuate your values and principles for generations to come. Whether it's instilling a strong work ethic, promoting environmental conservation, or advocating for social justice, your wealth can support initiatives and organizations that align with your beliefs.

3. Generational Wealth Transfer: Providing for Future Generations

Generational wealth transfer is the process of passing down wealth, assets, and financial wisdom to successive generations within your family. It involves not only the effective transfer of financial resources but also the cultivation of financial responsibility, stewardship, and a sense of purpose among your heirs.

A. Financial Education: An essential component of generational wealth transfer is providing financial education to your descendants. This education encompasses teaching them about financial principles, budgeting, investing, and responsible wealth management. By equipping your heirs with financial literacy, you empower them to make informed decisions and preserve family wealth.

B. Stewardship and Values: Passing on values and principles alongside financial resources is integral to generational wealth transfer. These values can include concepts of hard work, philanthropy, frugality, and responsible financial behavior. Encouraging your heirs to embrace these values helps ensure that wealth is managed wisely and used to create a positive impact.

C. Estate Planning: Effective estate planning is at the heart of generational wealth transfer. Establishing trusts, creating a well-structured will, and designating beneficiaries are essential steps to facilitate the smooth transition of assets to the next generation. It's crucial to involve legal and financial professionals in the estate planning process to address tax considerations and ensure that your wishes are accurately documented.

D. Open Communication: Open and transparent communication with your heirs is vital for the success of generational wealth transfer. Engaging in family discussions about financial matters, estate plans, and your expectations helps avoid misunderstandings and ensures that your heirs are well-prepared to handle their inheritance responsibly.

E. Philanthropic Values: If philanthropy is a significant part of your legacy, consider involving your heirs in charitable activities during your lifetime. This hands-on involvement can help them understand the impact of giving back and instill a sense of responsibility for continuing the family's philanthropic traditions.

F. Professional Guidance: Generational wealth transfer often involves complex legal, financial, and tax considerations. Seeking professional guidance from estate planning attorneys, financial advisors, and tax experts is essential to navigate these complexities effectively. These professionals can help you create a comprehensive plan that maximizes the benefits for both your heirs and charitable causes.

G. Wealth Preservation: To ensure the longevity of your generational wealth, consider strategies for wealth preservation. This may include establishing trusts that restrict access to principal funds until specific milestones or ages are reached, protecting assets from creditors or lawsuits, and incorporating tax-efficient strategies to minimize the impact of estate taxes.

Case Study: The Legacy of Generational Wealth

Let's explore a hypothetical case study to illustrate the concept of generational wealth transfer:

John, a successful entrepreneur, built a thriving business over several decades. Throughout his career, he practiced diligent financial management, diversified his investments, and prioritized saving for the future. As John approached retirement, he recognized the importance of preserving and transferring his wealth to benefit future generations.

1. Financial Education: John believed in the power of education and wanted to ensure that his grandchildren had access to quality higher education. He established a trust fund specifically designated for their college expenses. Alongside the trust, he initiated annual family gatherings where he shared stories of his financial journey, emphasizing the value of education and responsible money management.

2. Stewardship and Values: John instilled values of hard work, entrepreneurship, and philanthropy in his children and grandchildren. He encouraged them to pursue their passions and entrepreneurial endeavors while emphasizing the importance of giving back to their communities. By setting an example through his own charitable contributions and volunteer work, he inspired the next generations to embrace a spirit of generosity.

3. Estate Planning: John engaged an experienced estate planning attorney to create a comprehensive estate plan. This plan included a well-structured will, trusts for his heirs, and provisions for charitable donations to organizations close to his heart. He also established a family foundation that would continue to support charitable causes for generations to come.

4. Open Communication: Throughout his life, John maintained open and transparent communication with his family about financial matters. He regularly held family meetings to discuss the family's financial goals, the status of the family foundation, and the importance of responsible stewardship. These discussions helped foster a sense of unity and shared purpose among his heirs.

5. Philanthropic Values: John's commitment to philanthropy extended beyond his lifetime. He ensured that the family foundation had a clear mission statement and guidelines for grantmaking. He involved his children and grandchildren in the foundation's decision-making process, allowing them to contribute their insights and passions to charitable initiatives.

6. Professional Guidance: To navigate the complexities of generational wealth transfer and tax implications, John worked closely with financial advisors and estate planning experts. These professionals helped him optimize his estate plan to minimize tax liabilities and protect assets for future generations.

7. Wealth Preservation: John's estate plan included provisions to protect family assets from potential creditors or legal disputes. He also established a legacy fund within the family foundation, allocating a portion of the foundation's assets to support the ongoing costs of family gatherings, philanthropic initiatives, and financial education programs.

As a result of John's diligent efforts and thoughtful planning, his legacy of generational wealth continued to thrive long after his passing. His heirs not only benefited from the financial resources he had accumulated but also inherited a sense of responsibility, a commitment to education, and a passion for philanthropy. John's story exemplifies the potential for generational wealth transfer to create a lasting and positive impact on the lives of descendants and the broader community.

Estate Planning: Your Financial Roadmap

Estate planning is a critical component of wealth maintenance. It involves creating a comprehensive plan for the distribution of your assets upon your passing. Here are key elements of estate planning:

1. Will: Ensuring Your Legacy

A will, often referred to as a "last will and testament," is a foundational element of estate planning. It is a legal document that allows you to specify how your assets will be distributed after your death, providing clarity and direction to your loved ones and the legal system. A well-drafted will not only ensures your assets are distributed according to your wishes but also addresses important aspects such as guardianship for minor children and the appointment of an executor to oversee the process.

The Importance of a Will

A will serves several critical purposes in the estate planning process:

Asset Distribution: One of the primary functions of a will is to outline how your assets will be distributed among your heirs and beneficiaries. Without a will, your estate may be subject to the default rules of your state's intestacy laws, which may not align with your preferences.

Guardianship: If you have minor children, your will allows you to name guardians who will be responsible for their care in the event of your passing. This ensures that your children are placed under the care of individuals you trust.

Executor Appointment: A will typically designates an executor, often a trusted family member or friend, to carry out your wishes as outlined in the will. This person is responsible for managing your estate, paying debts, and distributing assets to beneficiaries.

Specific Bequests: A will allows you to make specific bequests, leaving particular assets or amounts to specific individuals or organizations. This can include sentimental items, monetary gifts, or charitable donations.

Debt Settlement: Your will can provide instructions for settling outstanding debts, taxes, and other financial obligations from your estate. This ensures that your assets are used efficiently to fulfill these obligations.

Avoiding Intestacy Laws: Perhaps most importantly, a will allows you to avoid the default distribution scheme established by your state's intestacy laws. These laws determine how assets are distributed when there is no valid will in place, often leading to unintended outcomes.

Key Considerations in Creating a Will

When creating a will, it's essential to consider the following aspects:

Executor Selection: Choose an executor who is reliable, organized, and capable of managing the responsibilities associated with settling your estate. It's advisable to discuss your choice with them beforehand to ensure they are willing to accept the role.

Asset Inventory: Compile a comprehensive list of your assets, including real estate, financial accounts, personal property, investments, and any valuable possessions. This inventory will guide the asset distribution process outlined in your will.

Beneficiary Designations: Be mindful of any assets with beneficiary designations, such as life insurance policies, retirement accounts, and bank accounts. These designations typically supersede the instructions in your will, so it's essential to review and update them as needed.

Specific Bequests: If you have specific items you wish to leave to particular individuals, clearly specify these in your will. This can help prevent disputes and ensure your wishes are carried out.

Guardianship for Minors: If you have minor children, carefully consider your choice of guardians. Discuss this decision with the chosen guardians to confirm their willingness and suitability for the role.

Review and Update: Your circumstances and preferences may change over time. It's crucial to periodically review and update your will to reflect these changes, ensuring it remains a true reflection of your wishes.

Legal Assistance: While it's possible to create a basic will on your own, seeking legal assistance from an estate planning attorney is advisable, especially if you have complex assets or unique considerations. An attorney can help ensure your will complies with state laws and is executed correctly.

2. Trusts: Enhanced Control and Flexibility

While a will is a fundamental tool in estate planning, trusts offer a higher degree of control, flexibility, and customization in wealth transfer. Trusts are legal arrangements that allow you to place assets in the care of a trustee, who manages and distributes those assets according to the terms you specify. Trusts can be tailored to address specific goals, such as providing for the long-term financial security of your loved ones, minimizing estate taxes, or supporting charitable causes.

Types of Trusts

There are various types of trusts, each serving distinct purposes and offering unique benefits. Some common types of trusts include:

Living Trust: Also known as a revocable trust, a living trust is created during your lifetime and can be altered or revoked as needed. It allows for the seamless transfer of assets to beneficiaries while avoiding the probate process.

Irrevocable Trust: An irrevocable trust, once established, typically cannot be modified or revoked without the consent of the beneficiaries. It offers potential tax benefits and asset protection.

Testamentary Trust: This type of trust is created through your will and takes effect upon your passing. It can be used to manage assets for minor children, disabled individuals, or beneficiaries with specific needs.

Charitable Trust: Charitable trusts are designed to benefit charitable organizations while providing potential tax advantages for the donor. They can be set up to provide income to the charity during your lifetime or to transfer assets to the charity upon your passing.

Special Needs Trust: A special needs trust is created to provide for the financial needs of individuals with disabilities while preserving their eligibility for government benefits.

Benefits of Using Trusts

Utilizing trusts in your estate plan can offer several advantages:

Probate Avoidance: Assets placed in a living trust can bypass the probate process, allowing for faster and more private distribution to beneficiaries.

Control and Flexibility: Trusts provide greater control over how and when assets are distributed. You can specify conditions or timing for distributions to beneficiaries.

Asset Protection: Irrevocable trusts can shield assets from creditors and legal claims, providing added protection for your beneficiaries.

Privacy: Unlike wills, which become public record during the probate process, trusts offer greater privacy since their details remain confidential.

Tax Efficiency: Certain types of trusts, such as charitable trusts and irrevocable life insurance trusts, can provide tax benefits for both you and your heirs.

Continuity: Trusts can ensure that your assets are managed and distributed as intended, even if you become incapacitated or after your passing.

Considerations in Establishing Trusts

When incorporating trusts into your estate plan, consider the following factors:

Trustee Selection: Carefully choose a trustee or trustees with the competence and integrity to carry out your wishes as outlined in the trust documents. You may appoint a family member, friend, or a professional trustee, depending on your preferences and the complexity of the trust.

Trust Funding: To be effective, a trust must be funded with assets. This involves transferring ownership of assets, such as real estate, financial accounts, or personal property, into the trust. Proper funding is essential to ensure that the trust serves its intended purpose.

Beneficiary Designations: Be mindful of how trust assets align with other beneficiary designations you may have on accounts such as retirement plans and life insurance policies. Coordinating beneficiary designations with the trust is crucial to avoid unintended conflicts.

Trust Terms: Clearly define the terms of the trust, including the conditions for distributions to beneficiaries, the timing of distributions, and any specific purposes or restrictions. These terms should align with your estate planning goals and intentions.

Legal Expertise: Given the complexity of trust structures and legal requirements, seeking the guidance of an experienced estate planning attorney is highly advisable. An attorney can assist in drafting trust documents that accurately reflect your wishes and comply with applicable state laws.

3. Beneficiary Designations: Ensuring Asset Alignment

In addition to creating a will and possibly establishing trusts, reviewing and updating beneficiary designations is a critical aspect of comprehensive estate planning. Beneficiary designations determine who will receive the assets held in specific accounts, such as life insurance policies, retirement accounts (e.g., 401(k)s and IRAs), and bank accounts. These designations often take precedence over instructions outlined in a will, making it essential to ensure they align with your overall estate planning goals.

The Importance of Beneficiary Designations

Beneficiary designations serve several key purposes in estate planning:

Asset Transfer: They specify the individuals or entities (such as charitable organizations) that will receive the assets in designated accounts upon your passing.

Probate Avoidance: Assets with valid beneficiary designations typically bypass the probate process, facilitating a quicker and more straightforward transfer to beneficiaries.

Privacy: Unlike wills, which become public record during probate, beneficiary designations remain private.

Continuous Asset Management: Assets held in accounts with beneficiary designations can continue to be managed and grow even after your passing, providing ongoing financial support to beneficiaries.

Potential Tax Benefits: Some beneficiary designations, such as those for retirement accounts, may offer tax advantages for beneficiaries.

Common Beneficiary Designations

Understanding the types of accounts and assets that typically involve beneficiary designations is essential:

Life Insurance Policies: Life insurance allows you to name one or more beneficiaries who will receive the death benefit upon your passing. You can designate individuals, trusts, or charitable organizations as beneficiaries.

Retirement Accounts: Retirement accounts, including 401(k)s, IRAs, and pension plans, require beneficiary designations. These designations determine how the account balance will be distributed to heirs or beneficiaries after your death.

Bank and Investment Accounts: Many financial institutions allow you to designate beneficiaries for accounts such as savings accounts, certificates of deposit (CDs), and brokerage accounts. This ensures a seamless transfer of these assets.

Annuities: If you own annuities, you can designate beneficiaries to receive any remaining annuity payments after your death.

Key Considerations in Beneficiary Designations

When managing beneficiary designations as part of your estate plan, consider the following:

Review and Update: Regularly review and update beneficiary designations to reflect changes in your life, such as marriage, divorce, births, deaths, or changes in your preferences. Outdated or incorrect designations can lead to unintended outcomes.

Primary and Contingent Beneficiaries: For each account, consider naming both primary and contingent (or secondary) beneficiaries. Primary beneficiaries receive the assets first, while contingent beneficiaries inherit them if the primary beneficiaries are deceased or unable to receive the assets.

Minors as Beneficiaries: If you intend to name minors as beneficiaries, consider establishing trusts or custodial accounts to manage their inheritances until they reach the age of majority. Naming minors directly can create complications.

Spousal Rights: Depending on your state's laws and the type of account, your spouse may have certain rights to the assets held within accounts with beneficiary designations. Be aware of these rights when making designations.

Simultaneous Death: Include provisions for the possibility that you and your designated beneficiaries may pass away simultaneously, such as in a common accident. These provisions may determine the next contingent beneficiaries or heirs.

Legal Guidance: Seek legal guidance from an estate planning attorney, especially when dealing with complex or high-value assets. An attorney can ensure that your beneficiary designations are aligned with your broader estate plan and legal requirements.

4. Power of Attorney: Empowering Trusted Decision-Making

A power of attorney (POA) is a legal document that grants another individual, known as the attorney-in-fact or agent, the authority to make financial and healthcare decisions on your behalf in the event you become incapacitated or unable to make these decisions independently. A well-structured POA is a fundamental component of comprehensive estate planning, as it provides guidance and continuity in managing your affairs when you are unable to do so yourself.

Types of Powers of Attorney

There are two primary types of powers of attorney:

Financial Power of Attorney: This document authorizes your chosen agent to handle financial matters on your behalf. These matters can include managing bank accounts, paying bills, conducting financial transactions, and even making decisions about buying or selling assets.

Healthcare Power of Attorney: A healthcare power of attorney, also known as a healthcare proxy or medical power of attorney, empowers your agent to make healthcare decisions for you when you are unable to do so. This can involve decisions about medical treatment, surgeries, medications, and end-of life care. It ensures that your medical preferences and values are respected, even if you cannot communicate them yourself.

The Importance of Powers of Attorney

Powers of attorney serve several crucial functions in estate planning and overall financial and healthcare management:

Decision Continuity: A power of attorney ensures the continuity of decision-making when you are unable to act. Without one, decisions about your finances and healthcare may be left to the courts, which can lead to delays and uncertainty.

Maintaining Financial Affairs: A financial power of attorney allows your agent to manage your financial affairs, pay bills, and access resources to support you and your dependents during times of incapacity.

Ensuring Healthcare Preferences: A healthcare power of attorney ensures that someone you trust is empowered to make healthcare decisions in alignment with your values and preferences. This can include decisions about life-sustaining treatments, organ donation, and the selection of medical providers.

Avoiding Conservatorship or Guardianship: Having a valid power of attorney in place can help avoid the need for court-appointed conservators or guardians. This can save time, money, and potentially prevent disputes among family members regarding who should manage your affairs.

Selecting Trusted Agents: Powers of attorney allow you to select individuals you trust to act on your behalf. These agents should be reliable, knowledgeable about your wishes, and willing to assume the responsibilities outlined in the documents.

Key Considerations in Establishing Powers of Attorney

When creating powers of attorney, consider the following:

Agent Selection: Choose your agents carefully. These individuals should have a clear understanding of your values, preferences, and priorities. They should also be capable of managing the responsibilities associated with their respective roles.

Clear Instructions: Provide clear instructions to your agents about your expectations and preferences. Discuss your wishes with them so they are prepared to act on your behalf in accordance with your values.

Financial Limits: You can establish specific financial limits or restrictions for your agent in your financial power of attorney. These limits can help prevent misuse of your assets.

Healthcare Directives: Ensure that your healthcare power of attorney aligns with any advance healthcare directives, living wills, or do-not-resuscitate (DNR) orders you may have in place. Clear communication with your healthcare agent is essential.

Successor Agents: In case your primary agent is unable or unwilling to act, consider naming successor agents who can step in if needed. This provides an additional layer of contingency planning.

Legal Review: Consult with an attorney experienced in estate planning to draft your powers of attorney. Different states may have specific requirements, and an attorney can ensure your documents comply with applicable laws.

5. Charitable Giving: Leaving a Lasting Impact

Charitable giving is a meaningful and impactful way to incorporate philanthropy into your estate plan. It allows you to support causes and organizations that are important to you, leaving a positive and lasting legacy. Whether you choose to make direct donations during your lifetime or include charitable provisions in your will or trust, your generosity can make a significant difference in the lives of others and contribute to the betterment of society.

Benefits of Charitable Giving

Charitable giving as part of your estate plan offers numerous benefits:

Fulfillment: Helping others and contributing to positive change in the world can bring a deep sense of fulfillment and purpose to your life. Knowing that your resources are making a difference can be highly rewarding.

Tax Advantages: Depending on your jurisdiction and the specific charitable giving methods you choose, there may be potential tax benefits, including income tax deductions and reduced estate taxes.

Legacy: By giving back, you leave a legacy of compassion, generosity, and positive change that continues to impact the world long after you're gone. Your values and commitment to making a difference endure through your charitable contributions.

Impact: Charitable giving allows you to support a wide range of causes and organizations that align with your values, from education and healthcare to environmental conservation and social justice.

Types of Charitable Giving

There are various ways to incorporate charitable giving into your estate plan:

Direct Donations: You can make direct donations to charitable organizations during your lifetime or through your will or trust. Cash, securities, real estate, and personal property are all assets that can be donated.

Charitable Trusts: Charitable remainder trusts (CRTs) and charitable lead trusts (CLTs) are legal structures that allow you to provide for both charitable and non-charitable beneficiaries. CRTs provide income to beneficiaries for a specified period, after which the remaining assets go to charity. CLTs, on the other hand, provide income to charities for a designated period before the remaining assets revert to non-charitable beneficiaries.

Donor-Advised Funds (DAFs): DAFs are philanthropic vehicles that allow you to make contributions to a fund established by a charitable sponsor. You can recommend grants from the fund to specific charities over time. DAFs offer flexibility and tax advantages.

Private Foundations: For those with significant wealth and a strong commitment to charitable giving, establishing a private foundation can provide a more direct and long-term approach to philanthropy. Private foundations require more administrative oversight but offer greater control over grantmaking.

Charitable Bequests: Including charitable bequests in your will or trust designates specific assets or a portion of your estate to go to charitable organizations upon your passing. This allows you to leave a legacy of support for causes that matter to you.

Key Considerations in Charitable Giving

When incorporating charitable giving into your estate plan, consider the following:

Identify Your Values: Determine the causes and organizations that are most meaningful to you. Consider your personal experiences, passions, and values when selecting charitable beneficiaries.

Research Charities: Thoroughly research charities to ensure they align with your values and effectively utilize donations for their intended purposes. Look for reputable organizations with a track record of impactful work.

Tax Implications: Understand the tax implications of your charitable contributions. Consult with a tax professional or financial advisor to optimize the tax benefits of your giving.

Asset Evaluation: Review your financial assets to identify assets that are suitable for charitable contributions.

You may choose to donate cash, appreciated securities, real estate, or other assets.

Consult Legal and Financial Experts: Seek advice from legal and financial experts, including estate planning attorneys and financial advisors, to ensure your charitable giving strategies align with your overall estate plan and financial goals.

Express Your Wishes: Clearly articulate your charitable intentions in your will, trust, or other relevant documents. This ensures that your charitable wishes are honored after your passing.

Regularly Review and Update: Periodically revisit your charitable giving plan to assess its alignment with your evolving values and financial circumstances. Make necessary adjustments to ensure your legacy continues to reflect your vision.

By thoughtfully incorporating these components—will, trusts, beneficiary designations, powers of attorney, and charitable giving—into your estate plan, you can establish a comprehensive and well-structured framework for the management and distribution of your assets, the protection of your interests, and the fulfillment of your philanthropic goals. Estate planning is a dynamic process that evolves with your life circumstances, so it's important to periodically review and update your plan to ensure it remains current and effective.

Your estate plan not only addresses the financial aspects of your legacy but also reflects your values, priorities, and the impact you wish to have on future generations and the causes you hold dear.

Retirement Planning: Enjoying Your Golden Years

Retirement planning is a key aspect of wealth maintenance. It involves saving and investing to ensure a comfortable and secure retirement. Here's how to approach retirement planning:
1. Define Retirement Goals: Crafting Your Ideal Retirement Lifestyle

Retirement is not just the absence of work; it's an opportunity to embrace a new chapter in life. To embark on this journey successfully, you need a roadmap. Defining your retirement goals is the first step in creating a fulfilling and financially secure retirement.

Retirement goals encompass various aspects of your future life:

Financial Security: How much income do you need to maintain your desired lifestyle and meet essential expenses? What is your desired standard of living in retirement?

Lifestyle Aspirations: What does your ideal retirement look like? Do you want to travel the world, spend more time with family, explore new hobbies, or engage in volunteer work?

Health and Wellness: Consider your healthcare needs and wellness goals. How will you maintain your physical and emotional well-being during retirement?

Legacy and Giving Back: Some individuals view retirement as an opportunity to give back to their communities or support causes they're passionate about. What legacy do you want to leave behind?

Defining Your Retirement Lifestyle

Begin by envisioning your retirement lifestyle. Imagine a typical day, week, or month in your retired life. What activities will you engage in? Where will you live? What experiences do you want to enjoy?

Next, consider the following factors:

Retirement Age: Determine the age at which you plan to retire. This can influence your retirement savings goals and the duration of your retirement.

Location: Think about where you want to live during retirement. Will you stay in your current home, downsize, move closer to family, or explore new destinations?

Financial Security: Estimate your financial needs in retirement. Calculate your expected expenses, including housing, healthcare, transportation, and discretionary spending.

Retirement Dreams: Identify your retirement dreams and aspirations. These can be travel adventures, pursuing hobbies, starting a new business, or dedicating more time to your passions.

Healthcare and Long-Term Care: Consider your healthcare needs and how you will address potential long-term care expenses.

Budgeting: Create a retirement budget that outlines your income sources, expenses, and savings goals. A budget is a practical tool to help you achieve your retirement goals.

Retirement Planning Milestones: Set specific milestones and goals for your retirement planning journey. These can include achieving a certain level of retirement savings, paying off debt, or finalizing your estate plan.

2. Retirement Accounts: Maximizing Your Savings Potential

Retirement accounts are instrumental in building the financial foundation for your retirement years. They offer tax advantages and, in many cases, employer contributions that can significantly boost your retirement savings. Here are some key retirement accounts to consider:

278

401(k) and 403(b) Plans: These employer-sponsored retirement plans are funded with pre-tax contributions. Contributions lower your taxable income, and the money grows tax-deferred until withdrawal. Many employers also offer matching contributions, which can substantially increase your savings.

Individual Retirement Accounts (IRAs): IRAs come in traditional and Roth varieties. Traditional IRAs allow tax-deductible contributions, while Roth IRAs offer tax-free withdrawals in retirement. Consider the tax implications and choose the right type for your circumstances.

SEP-IRA and SIMPLE IRA: If you're self-employed or own a small business, consider these retirement plan options. They allow you to make tax-deductible contributions for yourself and your employees.

457(b) Plans: These deferred compensation plans are available to certain government and non-profit employees. They offer pre-tax contributions and tax-deferred growth.

Maximizing Contributions:

To make the most of these retirement accounts, maximize your contributions. Here are some strategies to consider:

Contribute Up to the Limit: Contribute as much as you can, up to the annual contribution limits set by the IRS. These limits can change from year to year, so stay informed.

Catch-Up Contributions: Individuals age 50 and older can make catch-up contributions in addition to regular contributions. These catch-up contributions allow you to accelerate your retirement savings in the years leading up to retirement.

Employer Matching: If your employer offers a 401(k) match, contribute enough to maximize the match. This is essentially free money that can significantly boost your retirement savings.

Regular Contributions: Make contributions consistently throughout the year. Automatic contributions from your paycheck or bank account can help you stay on track.

Tax Benefits: Take advantage of the tax benefits associated with retirement accounts. For traditional 401(k) and IRA contributions, you may be able to deduct the contribution amount from your taxable income.

Tax Diversification: Consider diversifying your retirement savings between traditional and Roth accounts to give yourself flexibility in managing your tax liability during retirement.

3. Diversified Investments: Building a Resilient Portfolio

Investing is a critical component of retirement planning. It's a means to grow your wealth over time and generate income in retirement. While investing carries some level of risk, a well-diversified investment portfolio can help mitigate those risks and optimize returns.

Benefits of Diversification:

Diversification is the practice of spreading your investments across different asset classes and securities to reduce risk. Here

's why it's essential:

Risk Reduction: Diversification helps spread risk, reducing the impact of poor-performing assets on your overall portfolio. If one investment underperforms, others may compensate.

Steady Returns: Different asset classes have different performance patterns. By diversifying, you can potentially achieve more consistent returns over time.

Liquidity: Diversifying can improve liquidity by ensuring you have investments that can be easily converted to cash when needed.

Lower Volatility: A diversified portfolio tends to be less volatile than one concentrated in a single asset class. This can help you weather market downturns more effectively.

Types of Assets to Diversify:

Here are some common asset classes to consider when diversifying your investment portfolio:

Stocks: Equities represent ownership in companies and offer the potential for capital appreciation and dividends. Diversify your stock holdings across different industries and sectors to reduce risk.

Bonds: Bonds are debt securities that pay periodic interest and return the principal at maturity. They are relatively lower risk compared to stocks and can provide income stability.

Real Estate: Real estate investments involve purchasing properties for rental income or capital appreciation. Real estate can provide diversification and offer tax benefits.

Cash and Cash Equivalents: These include savings accounts, money market funds, and short-term CDs. Cash equivalents provide liquidity and stability but typically offer lower returns.

Alternative Investments: This category includes assets like commodities, hedge funds, and private equity. Alternative investments can provide additional diversification and returns uncorrelated with traditional asset classes.

International Investments: Consider diversifying internationally to access global markets and reduce risk associated with a single country's economic conditions.

Asset Allocation:

The key to effective diversification is asset allocation, which involves determining the right mix of asset classes for your portfolio. Your asset allocation should align with your risk tolerance, time horizon, and financial goals. It's essential to periodically review and rebalance your portfolio to maintain your desired asset allocation.

4. Healthcare Considerations: Preparing for Medical Expenses in Retirement

Healthcare is a significant expense in retirement, and planning for it is crucial to ensure your financial security and well-being. Here are some healthcare considerations to include in your retirement planning:

Medicare: Medicare is a federal health insurance program for individuals aged 65 and older. It consists of several parts, including hospital insurance (Part A), medical insurance (Part B), and prescription drug coverage (Part D). Understanding the different parts of Medicare and enrolling at the right time is essential to ensure you have adequate healthcare coverage.

Medigap or Medicare Advantage: Many retirees opt for supplementary insurance to cover the gaps in Medicare coverage.

Medigap policies and Medicare Advantage plans offer additional benefits and can help reduce out-of-pocket costs.

Long-Term Care Insurance: Long-term care insurance provides coverage for extended healthcare services, such as nursing home care or home healthcare. It can help protect your assets from being depleted by long-term care expenses.

Health Savings Accounts (HSAs): If you have a high-deductible health plan, you may be eligible for an HSA. HSAs offer tax advantages and can be used to save for healthcare expenses in retirement.

Budgeting for Healthcare: Estimate your healthcare costs in retirement and include them in your retirement budget. Consider factors such as premiums, deductibles, copayments, and potential long-term care expenses.

Maintaining Good Health: Prioritize your health and well-being to reduce healthcare expenses in retirement. Regular exercise, a healthy diet, and preventive care can contribute to lower healthcare costs.

5. Long-Term Care: Preparing for Future Healthcare Needs

Long-term care refers to a range of services and support needed by individuals with chronic illnesses or disabilities. These services may include assistance with activities of daily living, such as bathing, dressing, and eating. Planning for long-term care is an essential part of retirement planning, as it can significantly impact your financial well-being. Here's what you need to know:

Types of Long-Term Care: Long-term care can be provided in various settings, including nursing homes, assisted living facilities, and in your own home. The type of care you may need depends on your health condition and preferences.

Cost of Long-Term Care: Long-term care can be expensive, and costs vary based on location and the level of care required. It's essential to understand the potential financial impact and plan accordingly.

Long-Term Care Insurance: Long-term care insurance is designed to cover the costs of long-term care services. It can provide financial protection and help preserve your assets. Consider purchasing a long-term care insurance policy as part of your retirement planning strategy.

Self-Funding: Some individuals choose to self-fund their long-term care expenses by setting aside a portion of their retirement savings. While this approach provides flexibility, it also requires careful financial planning to ensure you have adequate resources.

Medicaid: Medicaid is a state and federally funded program that covers long-term care costs for individuals with limited financial resources. Eligibility criteria vary by state, and

it's essential to understand the rules and requirements.

Advance Directives: Consider creating advance directives, such as a healthcare power of attorney and living will, to specify your preferences for medical care in case you become unable to make decisions for yourself.

Family and Caregiving: Discuss long-term care plans and preferences with your family. Open communication can help ensure that your wishes are respected and that caregiving arrangements are in place if needed.

By addressing healthcare and long-term care considerations in your retirement planning, you can better prepare for potential expenses and make informed decisions about your financial security in retirement. Remember that healthcare needs can change over time, so regularly reviewing and adjusting your plan is essential to ensure it remains aligned with your goals and circumstances.

Generational Wealth Transfer: Passing on Your Legacy

Generational wealth transfer involves preserving and transferring wealth to future generations. It's not just about money; it's about passing on values, wisdom, and the responsibility of managing wealth responsibly. Here's how to approach generational wealth transfer:

1. Family Discussions: Engage in open and honest discussions with your family about wealth, values, and expectations. Create a shared understanding of your family's financial legacy.

2. Financial Education: Provide financial education and guidance to younger family members to prepare them for wealth stewardship.

3. Trusts and Foundations: Consider setting up trusts or family foundations to facilitate the transfer of assets and philanthropic activities.

4. Professional Advisors: Work with legal and financial professionals who specialize in estate planning and generational wealth transfer to ensure a seamless process.

Preserving Wealth for Future Generations

Preserving wealth for future generations requires a holistic approach that encompasses financial planning, education, and values transmission. Here are insights into effectively preserving wealth:

1. Financial Education: Educate younger generations about financial responsibility, investing, and wealth management. Equip them with the knowledge and skills to make informed decisions.

2. Instill Values: Pass on the values that have guided your financial journey, such as hard work, frugality, and philanthropy. Values can be the cornerstone of a family's financial legacy.

3. Philanthropy: Encourage and support philanthropic efforts among family members. Engaging in charitable activities can instill a sense of purpose and responsibility.

4. Regular Reviews: Periodically review and update your estate plan and generational wealth transfer strategy to adapt to changing circumstances and family dynamics.

Conclusion: A Lasting Financial Legacy

Wealth maintenance and longevity are the crowning achievements of the wealth mastery journey. They involve prudent planning, wise decision-making, and the desire to leave a lasting financial legacy. As you embark on this final phase of your journey, remember that wealth is not just about numbers; it's about the positive impact you can have on your own life and the lives of those who follow you.

By effectively managing and preserving your wealth, you can ensure a comfortable retirement, support charitable causes, and pass on a legacy of financial wisdom and responsibility. In doing so, you affirm the enduring power of wealth to create a better future for generations to come.

In the chapters that follow, we will conclude our journey with reflections on the lessons learned, the legacy we leave behind, and the infinite possibilities that lie ahead.

Chapter 11: Conclusion: The Road to Wealth Mastery

As we arrive at the final chapter of our journey, it's time to reflect on the road we've traveled, the knowledge we've gained, and the infinite possibilities that lie ahead. The path to wealth mastery is not merely a destination but a continuous journey—a journey marked by self-discovery, financial empowerment, and the pursuit of financial success. In this concluding chapter, we will summarize the key principles and strategies outlined in this book, encourage you to embark on your own journey to financial success, and convey the idea that wealth mastery is an ongoing process filled with growth and potential.

A Recap of Our Journey

Our journey to wealth mastery has been a comprehensive exploration of the principles, strategies, and mindset required to achieve financial success. Along this journey, we've covered a wide range of topics, each contributing to a holistic understanding of wealth:

1. Defining Wealth: We began by redefining wealth beyond money, recognizing its psychological and emotional aspects. We emphasized that wealth encompasses a rich and fulfilling life.

2. Goal Setting and Financial Planning: We discussed the significance of setting clear financial goals and provided strategies for effective financial planning. We explored examples of successful individuals who achieved their financial goals through focused planning.

3. The Wealth Mindset: We delved into the mindset and attitudes that contribute to wealth creation. We discussed common mental barriers to financial success and shared personal stories of individuals who transformed their mindset.

288

4. Income Generation Strategies: We detailed various income sources and strategies for increasing earning potential. We highlighted the importance of diversification and offered actionable advice for career advancement, entrepreneurship, and passive income streams.

5. Smart Saving and Investing: We explained the principles of saving and investing wisely. We provided insights into different investment vehicles, such as stocks, real estate, and retirement accounts, and discussed risk management and long-term wealth accumulation.

6. Debt Management and Financial Freedom: We addressed the role of debt in wealth building and how to manage it effectively. We shared strategies for debt reduction and achieving financial independence by living below your means and building a savings cushion.

7. Building Multiple Income Streams: We explored the concept of creating multiple income streams for financial security. We highlighted the gig economy, side hustles, and investments as avenues for additional income and provided case studies of individuals who diversified their income sources.

8. Legacy and Philanthropy: We discussed the importance of leaving a financial legacy and explored philanthropic opportunities. We showcased stories of individuals who made a meaningful impact through their wealth.

9. Navigating Economic Challenges: We addressed economic downturns, recessions, and financial setbacks. We provided strategies for resilience and recovery during tough times and shared real-life stories of individuals who thrived despite adversity.

10. Wealth Maintenance and Longevity: We emphasized the importance of maintaining and growing wealth over time. We offered guidance on estate planning, retirement, and generational wealth transfer. We shared insights into preserving wealth for future generations.

A New Beginning

As we conclude this journey, it's important to recognize that the knowledge and strategies you've gained are not just theoretical concepts but practical tools for shaping your financial future. Whether you are just starting your journey or are well on your way, the principles of wealth mastery are timeless and adaptable to your unique circumstances.

Embrace the Journey: The journey to wealth mastery is not a one-size-fits-all path. It's a deeply personal and evolving process. Embrace it with enthusiasm, knowing that every step you take brings you closer to your financial goals.

Continuous Learning: Just as our journey together doesn't end here, neither does your pursuit of financial success. Wealth mastery is an ongoing process of learning, adapting, and growing. Stay curious and open to new opportunities.

Share Your Knowledge: As you progress on your journey, consider sharing your knowledge and experiences with others. Whether it's through mentoring, teaching, or philanthropy, passing on what you've learned can have a lasting impact.

Live a Rich Life: While the accumulation of wealth is an important aspect of financial success, remember that wealth is a means to an end, not the end itself. Ultimately, it's about living a rich and fulfilling life, pursuing your passions, and contributing to the well-being of others.

Conclusion: Your Wealth Mastery Awaits

As we part ways, I encourage you to embark on your journey to
financial success with confidence and determination. The
principles and strategies you've discovered are the building blocks
of a prosperous future. Wealth mastery is within your reach, and
the road ahead is filled with opportunities for growth, prosperity,
and the realization of your financial dreams.

So, take the first step, set your goals, and begin your journey
today. Remember that the pursuit of wealth mastery is not a
destination but a lifelong adventure. It's about the continuous
evolution of your financial well-being, the empowerment that
comes with knowledge, and the fulfillment of your aspirations.

Thank you for joining me on this remarkable journey. May your
path to wealth mastery be filled with abundance, wisdom, and the
joy of financial success.

The End of "Your Wealth Mastery Journey"

Appendices: Resources for Wealth Building

In your journey to wealth mastery, knowledge is your most powerful tool. To support your ongoing learning and practical application of the principles and strategies outlined in this book, we've compiled a valuable collection of resources. In this appendices chapter, you will find a list of recommended books, websites, and tools for further learning. Additionally, we've included worksheets and templates to assist you in your financial planning and goal setting, ensuring that you have the practical resources needed to embark on your path to financial success.

Recommended Reading

Books have long been a source of wisdom and inspiration in the field of personal finance and wealth building. Here is a selection of recommended books that cover a wide range of financial topics:

1. **"The Millionaire Next Door" by Thomas J. Stanley and William D. Danko:** This classic explores the habits and lifestyles of wealthy individuals, shedding light on their frugal and disciplined approach to wealth.

2. **"Rich Dad Poor Dad" by Robert Kiyosaki:** A transformative book that challenges conventional wisdom about money and offers insights into building wealth through assets and entrepreneurship.

3. **"The Total Money Makeover" by Dave Ramsey:** A practical guide to financial freedom, offering a step-by-step plan for eliminating debt and achieving financial goals.

4. **"Your Money or Your Life" by Vicki Robin and Joe Dominguez:** This book provides a comprehensive program for

transforming your relationship with money and achieving financial independence.

5. **"The Little Book of Common Sense Investing" by John C. Bogle:** A guide to passive investing and the power of low-cost index funds, written by the founder of Vanguard Group.

6. **"The Bogleheads' Guide to Investing" by Taylor Larimore, Mel Lindauer, and Michael LeBoeuf:** A comprehensive resource on investing inspired by the principles of John Bogle.

7. **"The Richest Man in Babylon" by George S. Clason:** A timeless classic that imparts financial wisdom through a collection of parables set in ancient Babylon.

Websites and Online Resources

In the digital age, an abundance of online resources can enhance your financial knowledge and decision-making. Here are some websites and online platforms to explore:

1. **Investopedia:** An extensive resource for financial education, offering articles, tutorials, and a comprehensive financial dictionary.

2. **Bogleheads:** A community of investors inspired by the principles of John Bogle, offering forums, guides, and resources on investing and personal finance.

3. **The Motley Fool:** A website providing investment advice, stock recommendations, and educational content for investors of all levels.

4. **Khan Academy:** Offers free, high-quality courses on personal finance and investing, making complex financial concepts accessible to everyone.

5. **Mint:** A personal finance app that helps you budget, track expenses, and manage your financial goals.

6. **Morningstar:** Provides investment research, data, and analysis on a wide range of investment products and strategies.

Financial Planning Worksheets and Templates

Effective financial planning is essential for achieving your wealth-building goals. Here are downloadable worksheets and templates to assist you in your financial planning journey:

1. **Budget Worksheet:** Use this template to create a monthly budget, track income and expenses, and gain a clear overview of your financial situation.

2. **Goal Setting Worksheet:** Set specific, measurable, achievable, relevant, and time-bound (SMART) financial goals using this worksheet.

3. **Debt Payoff Plan:** Create a plan to pay off your debts systematically, including credit card debt, student loans, and more.

4. **Investment Portfolio Tracker:** Monitor and manage your investment portfolio with this template, tracking asset allocation and performance.

5. **Retirement Savings Calculator:** Estimate how much you need to save for retirement and calculate the contributions required to reach your retirement goals.

6. **Estate Planning Checklist:** A comprehensive checklist to guide you through the estate planning process, including wills, trusts, and beneficiary designations.

Conclusion: Empowering Your Wealth Journey

As you explore the recommended resources and utilize the financial planning worksheets and templates provided in this appendices chapter, remember that knowledge alone is not enough. It's the practical application of this knowledge that will empower your wealth journey.

Wealth mastery is not a destination; it's a continuous process of learning, planning, and taking action. Use these resources to refine your financial strategy, set meaningful goals, and make informed decisions. As you navigate the complexities of wealth building, remember that your journey is unique, and your financial success is within reach.

Acknowledgments and Author Bio

Acknowledgments

The journey to create this book, "Your Wealth Mastery Journey," has been a collaborative effort, and it's with profound gratitude that I acknowledge the individuals and forces that contributed to its realization.

First and foremost, I want to express my deepest appreciation to my family for their unwavering support and understanding during the countless hours spent researching, writing, and refining this book. Your encouragement and belief in my mission have been my greatest motivation.

I extend my heartfelt thanks to my friends and colleagues who provided valuable insights, feedback, and encouragement throughout the writing process. Your perspectives and enthusiasm have enriched this book and strengthened my resolve to empower others on their wealth mastery journey.

A special mention goes to the dedicated team of editors, designers, and publishing professionals who worked tirelessly to transform my ideas into a polished and reader-friendly book. Your expertise and commitment to excellence have been instrumental in bringing this project to fruition.

To the mentors and teachers who have imparted wisdom and knowledge along my own journey to financial literacy, I am profoundly grateful. Your guidance has not only shaped my understanding of wealth but also inspired me to share these insights with a broader audience.

Finally, I extend my gratitude to you, the reader. It is your curiosity, your thirst for knowledge, and your determination to master the art of wealth that make this book a meaningful endeavor. My hope is that the pages ahead will serve as a valuable resource on your own path to financial success.

Author Bio

Allow me to introduce myself. I am Eric Ornelas, the author of "Your Wealth Mastery Journey." My passion for personal finance and wealth building was ignited early in life, driven by a desire to understand the mechanics of financial success and share that understanding with others.

My journey toward financial literacy has been a dynamic one, marked by continuous learning and a commitment to staying informed about the ever-evolving landscape of personal finance. I firmly believe that financial empowerment is within reach for everyone, and it's this belief that inspired me to write "Your Wealth Mastery Journey."

Throughout my career, I have had the opportunity to work with great minds to bring to you this book. These experiences have deepened my understanding of wealth creation and the multifaceted aspects of financial well-being.

In addition to my professional pursuits, I am an advocate for selling shoes. I firmly believe that wealth mastery not only benefits individuals but also has the power to create positive ripple effects in communities and society as a whole.

When I'm not immersed in the world of finance, you can find me playing hoops at my local basketball club. These pursuits bring balance to my life and remind me of the importance of both financial and personal well-being.

I am excited to share the knowledge, strategies, and insights within this book to empower you on your own journey to financial success. My hope is that the principles and practical guidance provided will serve as a valuable resource as you embark on the path to wealth mastery.

Thank you for joining me on this transformative journey, and I look forward to being your guide as we explore the wealth-building principles that can change your financial future.